Happiness D

Strength of will, against all odds

RAFAEL SANTANDREU

&

PETE PALLARÉS

Rafael Santandreu & Pete Pallarés

ISBN: 978-1-965408-06-3
Published by [Book Writing League]

Acknowledgment

"To all those who pick up this book, thank you for giving our words a chance." "For all readers who find themselves within these chapters." For every person, who find the path to follow." To the ones reading this, may you find the courage, determination, and love contained within these pages, this book is for you"

"The reason happiness is not out there somewhere for us to find is because happiness is ...inside us. Becoming continues to be much better than being"

"To Perla and Penélope Pallarés, this book is dedicated to you...shine, the world is waiting for you."

"The reason happiness is not out there somewhere for us to find is because happiness is ...inside us. Becoming continues to be much better than being"

"To Perla and Penelope Pallarés, this book is dedicated to you...shine, the world is waiting for you."

Rafael Santandreu & Pete Pallarés

Table of Contents

Happiness Declassified

Foreword

I have been dedicated to psychotherapy for 30 years and I know that cognitive (or cognitive-behavioral) psychology is the main key to mental transformation. I myself experienced a vital comeback at the age of 25 when I discovered it. I went from being overwhelmed, anxious, and disgusted with the world to simply HAPPY. And it only took me a month to achieve almost all that happiness. A month of super intense work with my internal dialogue, my personal philosophy, and my beliefs about the world. It's incredible but true. I know that you can achieve the same if you apply what this book says to the fullest. I have also verified it in thousands of patients that I have been fortunate enough to treat. I'm going to ask you a favor. When you, too have made that wonderful change, contact me or Pete and tell us your story. We love these stories. So much so that on my official YouTube channel, we post video interviews every week with people like you or me, who, after reading this book, have changed everything. Now they are delighted with life and know how to explain how they have achieved it. I'll wait for you. Sending you a warm hug,

Rafael Santandreu

Happiness Declassified

I have the great pleasure of presenting this great work, whose main author is not only a colleague but also a great friend. Although I greatly appreciate all of Rafael Santandreu's work as a brilliant writer and psychologist, it's important that I confess my preference for this one, not only because I'm part of the creative process but because this book allows us to impact many more lives around the world. When Rafael approached me with the idea of collaborating on something aimed at an English-speaking audience, I felt not only a great level of humility but also a tremendous fascination with the idea of becoming the co-author of one of his books. What an honor! After more than 30 years as a therapist, businessman, athlete, musician, and philanthropist, I find Happiness Declassified a basic instrument to understand the principles of cognitive psychology and the path to happiness. I hope you enjoy this work and, above all, find the reading we present to you as useful and enjoyable as much as I have enjoyed co-authoring it and collaborating with Rafael Santandreu.

Pete Pallarés

Part One:
Understanding Cognitive Therapy
1
Programming the Mind

Among the ancient pigmy people, this story is told:

> *One day, a thirsty lion came to a lake of clear water,*
> *and as he dipped his head to drink, he saw his*
> *reflection for the first time. Alarmed, he thought,*
> *"This lake is that fierce lion's territory. I'd better*
> *leave!"*

But the lion was very thirsty, so a few hours later, he decided to return. He snuck up to the lake and, just as he bent his neck to drink, there his new rival was! He couldn't believe it! How could this damned animal be so fast and so alert?

What could he do? He was dying of thirst, and it was the only source of water for miles around. Desperate, it occurred to him to go around the lake to a dark corner. When he arrived there, he crept up to the water and... bam! The same jaws were in front of him! He despaired. Never had he faced such a territorial adversary...

But the lion was so thirsty he decided to go for broke. He mustered his courage, ran to the shore, and without thinking about it, thrust his head into the water. That was when, as the pigmy elders recount, the magic happened: his ferocious rival had disappeared forever!

More than sixteen years ago, I had an incredible, beautiful experience that had a huge impact on me: I stopped smoking. And I didn't do it just any old how, but using the best method in the world, without going "cold turkey," enjoying the process, even. It was like a miracle – the first miracle I witnessed in the universe of psychology – though later, through my work, I would witness a great many more.

Before I found the right method, I'd tried twice to give up, both times ending in memorable failure. The longest I lasted without smoking was a couple of hours! Straight after quitting, I would climb the walls until I told myself, "I can't do it anymore. I'd rather die of cancer than suffer this terrible anxiety!"

But then I had the enormous good fortune of stumbling across Allen Carr's book *The Easy Way to Stop Smoking*. This Scottish accountant had managed to find a way to give up smoking effortlessly, using some fabulous mental programming.

The most amazing thing about his method is that it makes it possible to quit smoking without suffering any withdrawal symptoms – none! And this, although, until now, medical science has taken it for granted that addictive drugs cause a powerful "cold turkey" feeling when the person withdraws. It's assumed that a heroin addict will always have a tough time trying to detox from the drug: contortions, stomach pains, sweating, and even delirium for several days.

But this Scotsman with no medical knowledge – he wasn't even a psychologist – argued that there's no such thing as the "cold turkey," that it's all in our minds. I've been able to confirm that he was right, and I'm not the only one to have experienced this phenomenon! Thousands of people around the world have reprogrammed their brains using the Allen Carr method and managed to give up their terrible addiction without difficulty.

In fact, a month after I gave up smoking, my mother, a heavy smoker for thirty years, asked me for "that little book that helped you so much." And a week later, she, too was throwing her last cigarette in the bin. More than sixteen years on, if there's one thing clear in her mind, it's that that poison will never touch her lips again. Her experience was identical to mine! And she didn't find it hard. She even enjoyed the process! But you might be wondering why I'm talking about smoking in a psychology book whose purpose is to help us grow stronger on an emotional level. Well, for no other reason than the fact that all mental states – anxiety, depression, stress, shyness, etc. – are also smoke; that is, they're merely the product of errors in thinking, which we can reverse, quickly and permanently, using the right method.

I will show you that, as Allen Carr said about smoking, emotional change is "easy when you know how."

This book is a manual for mental reprogramming similar to Allen Carr's system for giving up smoking but applied to all negative emotions. In fact, it could easily be entitled, "It's easy to stop having hang-ups if you know how." Its purpose is to transform its readers into people with excellent emotional health. The methods explained here are based on cognitive psychology, the most effective therapeutic approach in the world, with thousands of studies that demonstrate its results. And the best thing about these methods is that anyone can make use of them. In other words, nobody needs to see a psychologist if they make the necessary effort.

Being Brilliant

What are we going to become after adopting the methods in this book? Well, nothing more and nothing less than special people – strong and healthy human beings. Nowadays, due to a prevailing neurosis, just 20 % of people achieve this. If you work mindfully with this book, you will be able to transform yourself into an individual who is highly focused on the present.

I once heard someone say, "A good monk is one who doesn't do many things, but the few things he does, he does very well." When you're in good mental shape, the day flows naturally, from pleasure to pleasure. Because you'll find opportunities to do something wonderful everywhere, and the *sweet present* will be where you reside regardless of your mental state.

When we're vulnerable, we distinguish between being "fine" and being "down in the dumps" because we experience negative emotions in an extreme way. Yet the healthiest people experience the negative things in a very mild way. They even know how to enjoy a little sadness or some energizing nerves. Essentially, they're very stable and know how to observe reality through the eyes of a poet.

With cognitive therapy, your eye for beauty is activated, enabling you to notice the beautiful things around you much more often and in a better way: nice faces, a city's giant trees… there are few things that provide more fulfilment than appreciating the little pleasures in life with intensity and being grateful just to be alive. This will begin to happen continually, in a spontaneous way.

A happy person has charisma and power of attraction because "good vibes" are contagious, and everybody wants to be near them. And people bursting with happiness show the best side of themselves, which also makes them very attractive.

So, we have to say *yes*, it *is* possible to free ourselves from fear. In fact, it's easier than it seems. And then life becomes something incredibly simple. On top of that, when we banish our fears, we gain a huge competitive advantage. Strong and happy people enjoy many more opportunities simply because they're ready for anything, while the majority are held back by absurdities.

I stopped smoking in a radical way and without effort – I even enjoyed the process. And in the same way, I've seen thousands of people transform themselves into that special human being that I've just described. The changes are truly amazing.

Outside of cognitive therapy, I've only seen such radical changes in people who have converted to a religion and experience it in a profound way. More than once, I've heard descriptions like, "She was the same person, but there was something different in her eyes: they were bright – sparkling, even."

Marcus was one of these people. He was a young German I met in my youth who worked as a volunteer in an Indian slum. Marcus had left everything behind in his native Munich to join a protestant religious order in Calcutta. This tall, blonde, determined twenty-year-old's eyes were also sparkling. His life force was as clean and as joyful as I've ever seen. That's what I call emotionally fit!

A Super-Intense Workout

This is the third book I've published, and in the five years that bookshops have stocked my manuals, I've received thousands of letters from people who've experienced a powerful transformation through the cognitive method. People who were depressed, anxious, ultra-jealous, obsessive, or fearful to the point of paralysis have managed to forge another mind, something they didn't even know was possible.

This third book aims to go a step further, to develop more intensity in your reprogramming. The goal is to become an exceptionally healthy person – a rarity in this crazy world. The objective is to become very healthy and very strong, with a clear, brilliant mind like Marcus's.

In this chapter we learned that:

- The effectiveness of the cognitive method has been proven hundreds of times over by independent evaluators.
- It involves very powerful mental reprogramming that makes the seemingly difficult easy.
- The aim is to become exceptional people: calm, focused on the present, happy even during illness, with a poet's eyes, attractive outside and in, and free from fear.

2
A Three-Step System

When the sun rose on the appointed day, the Christians marched in procession in the direction of the Roman amphitheater. Yet, as if parading towards heaven rather than being thrown to the hounds, their faces were alight with joy.

The people packed the streets to see them pass by, but surprisingly, without the usual revelry with which such street entertainment was received. This time, nobody threw rotten vegetables; no insults could be heard. The Romans were intrigued – alarmed, even – by these eccentrics who worshipped a man executed on a cross.

That morning, on the way to the amphitheater, all that could be heard was the cowardly murmur of the people speaking in low voices.

Finally, the party reached the imposing Colosseum. Inside, some officials awaited them, who covered them in bloody rabbit skins to excite the dogs that would devour them later on.

Dressed in this way, the group went out onto the sand. The crowd, hungry for the spectacle of death, erupted into jeers. Fierce hounds drooled at three equidistant points of the arena. Amid the noise, a large group of spectators began to chorus, "Death to the pagans! Death to the pagans!" It was a chant like those of modern football stadiums. The word "pagan" obviously referred to the Christians, who spurned the vast catalog of Roman gods.

The condemned, who included children with their feet in chains, headed to the center of the enclosure as they had been instructed. In their positions, the dogs pulled on their chains, eager to feed.

But as the believers headed towards certain death, a sound never heard before began to ring out: it was a beautiful melody of voices. Many Romans stopped shouting to listen to it. As the masses fell silent, the melody became clear: it was the Christians themselves intoning the song. The crowds could not believe what they were hearing! These strange people were serene. What's more, their faces glowed. Some of them embraced as if saying goodbye but with no tears or wailing.

The official in charge of the games, Julius Pontius, a bald, obese man, was taking cover behind a wooden barrier. Nervously, he looked at the emperor and saw an expression of annoyance. He quickly gestured to the dog trainers and yelled, "Release the hounds! What are you waiting for, imbeciles!"

And on that command, the savage animals shot off in the direction of the Christians. When they reached their prey, the crazed roar of the people broke out in the amphitheater once more. Nero and Julius Pontius breathed a sigh of relief. But the seed of curiosity and admiration had already been planted in the minds of the people. All week, no one could stop talking about the Christians.

In 64 ADS, a great fire took hold of Rome. Seventy percent of the city, which had a million inhabitants at the time, was engulfed in flames.

Rome was heated and lit with firewood, and the city was a chaotic mass of narrow streets crammed with shops and apartment buildings on several floors, so fires were commonplace, but this one was of gigantic proportions.

Rumors circulated at the time that the fire had been started intentionally because it began in the very neighborhood where the emperor was planning to build a new palace. Nero may have wanted to clear the area without having to pay compensation. This corrupt madman was capable of anything…

When the whispers reached the palace, an anxious Nero prepared a propagandist response – if he could make the people believe that the disaster was the work of the Christians, he could calm things down with an exemplary punishment. And his plan worked. Rome took the bait, and the Christians were massacred. A year later, a new palace was erected on the charred plot of land.

Thus began the first persecution of the Christians, a state crime that, ultimately, would come back to bite the Roman institutions. As the historians of the time recount, those condemned for the new religion showed such strength that their punishment became a powerful publicity campaign in their favor.

It has been recorded that many of those Christians died in the Roman arena, calm, confident, and surreally serene. The citizens of Rome asked themselves, "What does this foreign faith have which gives its believers such uncommon moral superiority?" And that was the best publicity Christianity could have received.

The renowned Roman philosopher Justin was one of these people who converted to the religion of the cross after being moved by the phenomenon of the martyrs. He wrote:

> *When I was a disciple of Plato, hearing the accusations made against the Christians and seeing them intrepid in the face of death and of all that men fear, I said to myself that it was impossible that they should be living in evil and in the love of pleasure.*

The historian Tertullian wrote:

> *Many men, marveling at their courageous perseverance, sought the causes for such a strange and powerful mood, and when they knew the truth, they converted to the new religion.*

I'm not a Catholic, but the story of these people facing martyrdom with serenity and joy seems like the perfect example of how the mind can be trained for any situation. Even to the point of going to one's death with joy!

Everything is in the mind, for better or worse. This fact can be our friend or our enemy. It's something that I have witnessed at my practice for many years, and in extreme forms such as somatization – bodily symptoms created by the mind. These people come to me with extraordinary conditions like paralysis, chronic pain, or even blindness caused by a dysfunction of the mind.

But I know that the opposite can also happen: lucky people with a bomb-proof mind whom nothing prevents from being happy – not serious illness, not prison, not war.

Cognitive psychology teaches us that, with a little effort and perseverance, we can all move towards having the mindset of the strongest people. Sometimes, it will be very quick and easy; sometimes, it will require a few years of training. It depends on where we start from. But it is the most important kind of learning because our central computer, the mind, controls everything.

Escaping Hell in Twenty Sessions

One example of the radical change I'm describing is Alejandra. Her father called me from Zaragoza, where he owned a thriving chain of electrical appliance shops. He explained to me that his 33-year-old daughter had the family in despair. From the age of sixteen, she had suffered from what is known as *borderline personality disorder*. Psychiatrists use this term to describe people prone to depression and anxiety, with tendencies towards suicide and self-harm. They often cut their arms to feel physical instead of emotional pain, which is not uncommon when a person reaches such levels of suffering.

Alejandra's father asked me to accept his daughter as a patient and so I did. The young woman had just come out of a prestigious psychiatric clinic in Madrid, admitted for the umpteenth time, and the family was despondent because she was returned to them stuffed full of pills and with no prospect of getting better.

Less than a year later, after twenty visits to my practice in Barcelona, Alejandra was a different person. Not only was she happy and radiant but, as her father told me through tears, "She must be the strongest person in the family." She no longer took medication, she was working – in the family business – for the first time in her life, and she was planning to move in with a young man she'd met. She was elated!

Changes like this are not miracles – they are simply the result of learning with a clear method and with a lot of hard work and perseverance. It's a bit like learning a foreign language: practice makes perfect.

The Power of The Mind

I have a very strong and rational friend, who I've mentioned several times in my books. Her name is Tina Pereyre. She's the volunteer manager at the Sant Joan de Déu Hospital in Barcelona, one of Spain's largest children's hospitals.

Fiercely Christian, genuine, and energetic, she is always cheerful. A delightful person who radiates love wherever she goes. A friend once told me a story about her that illustrates the power of mental attitude. Tina was going through an especially difficult time in her life – she had separated from her husband, one of her daughters was seriously ill, etc. – and when her friends asked her, "Tina, how are you?"

She would respond, "Outside or inside?"

"I don't know, both," they would usually say.

"Outside, bad because so many bad things are happening to me, but inside, I'm happy," she would conclude.

So, what's the secret to developing this kind of emotional strength? What is the key to freeing oneself from any fear, complex, or psychological problem? Cognitive therapy has the answer. It consists of three steps:

1. Looking inwards (seeking well-being inside oneself)

2. Learning to travel light (knowing how to let go of everything)

3. Appreciating what's around you (learning to have a passion for life)

If we can master these three steps, we can free ourselves of any hang-ups and become very strong and happy. The best version of ourselves.

Let's take a quick look at what these three skills consist of. However, bear in mind this is just an outline – over the course of the book, we'll look at them in much more detail.

Step one: looking inward

The main reason human beings are neurotic is that we believe that happiness comes from the outside. This is the biggest error that makes a mess of our brains.

We make this mistake every time we say, "When I find a partner, I'll be able to enjoy life," or, "If I didn't have this cancer, I could be happy," or, "If I was more beautiful, my life would take off." All of this is a misconception because the main activator for happiness is inside us, not in our external reality. And failing to realize this – over and over – is the seed for emotional weakness.

Alejandra, my "borderline" patient, was a master of this error. Before she got better, virtually anything could be a reason to feel depressed or anxious: not having a boyfriend, a friend mistreating her, getting bored, the possibility of falling ill… And that, in fact, was the same as saying that happiness was the opposite: having a boyfriend, being treated well, having an exciting life, or being healthy…

In contrast, my friend Tina didn't pay much attention to external things. Inside, she was always calm and happy, regardless of her problems. That's why the first step to being emotionally strong is to focus on our mental processes and less on external things.

Every time we feel disturbed, we can ask ourselves: "What have I done to feel like this?" If a workmate says something unpleasant to us and we feel offended, it's not because of the offense itself but because of our internal dialogue – what we tell ourselves when difficulties arise. Instead of looking outside, we must look inside.

When we're weak, we make the mistake of paying too much attention to our circumstances. Stupidly, we become prisoners of these circumstances, slaves to the things that happen. Epictetus, one of the philosophers who underpins cognitive psychology, said, "We are not affected by what happens to us, but by what we tell ourselves about what happens to us."

As we will learn throughout this book, we will change by saying to ourselves, in any situation: "Being okay or not okay depends on my thinking, not on my problems or successes."

Step two: learning to travel light

There was once a traveler in Israel who wanted to meet the celebrated rabbi Hillel the Elder. When he stepped into his house, he was surprised to see that it consisted of just one room filled with books, with a single stool to sit on.

The traveler asked, "But Rabbi, where is your furniture?"

"Where is yours?" asked the wise man.

"I'm just passing through…"

"And what do you think I'm doing?" the rabbi concluded.

The true cause of unhappiness is believing that we lack things. Conversely, the key to well-being is to know that we have more than enough of everything. It's what I call "living in a state of abundance" or "living in a state of want."

On innumerable occasions, I've asked a patient, "Do you realize you have everything you need to be happy?" Sometimes, it's a young woman whose boyfriend has left her; sometimes, a cancer sufferer or people with anxiety or chronic pain. And the treatment begins to work when they realize that adversity is not an obstacle to being happy. Just ask the Christian martyrs!

Behind every neurosis – every single one of them – there is always an inability to let go of one's *invented needs*, a demand. Always! And the solution is to let it go by understanding that we do not truly need whatever it is. As I always say, neuroses are caused by "a state of need," the belief that we need much more than we really do in order to be okay.

A while ago, I watched an interview with Andreu Buenafuente's famous TV show host in Spain (available on YouTube), which illustrates this concept. The guest was Jorge Sánchez, a writer who held the record for journeys around the world. He'd spent thirty-five of his fifty years traveling. He seemed like a great guy: interesting, serene, fun, and full of energy and curiosity. Sánchez explained that he traveled with very little money, working here and there however he could, gathering experiences and friends. He'd had all kinds of adventures and misadventures – even narrowly avoiding death – but he'd never stopped being immensely happy.

This man travels light in life, and he is an example of emotional strength and good health.

The strongest people – rich or poor – have reduced their needs to very low levels. They might have a mansion, a wonderful partner, and an enviable job, but they know that they don't need any of that. If at any time they're left without it, they remain as happy as before.

The pyramid of relinquishment

Listed below are the five fundamental relinquishments that must be made to become a healthy person. I've framed them in a pyramid of ascending difficulty. Every day, as a reminder, we can make a commitment to them. I can promise you that if you can persuade yourself that you don't need these key assets, you will become an exceptionally healthy person. It's no coincidence that every strong person has managed to do it, from my former patient from Zaragoza to Jorge Sánchez, the happy traveler.

The first relinquishment, the most basic, is financial security. The aim is to grasp that we can be perfectly happy without money – provided, of course, that we have food and drink covered. If we're unable to see ourselves being okay if we lose our job, we'll always be afraid of losing what we have, we'll get stressed easily and we won't be able to enjoy our work to the full.

Some time ago, I released myself completely from a need for financial security, and that is my secret to a stress-free life. Paradoxically, it's what enabled me to be successful.

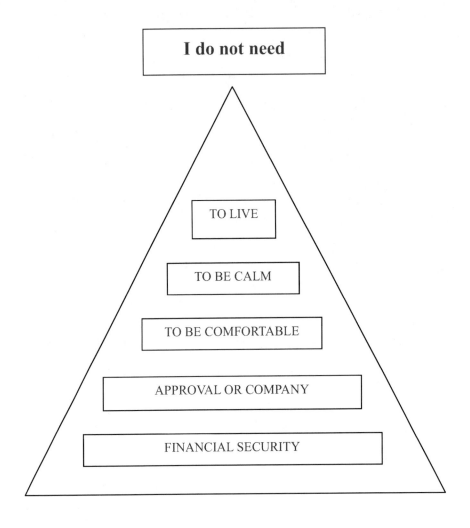

As we will learn over the course of this book, whenever work-related stress emerges, or a report or meeting with the boss fills us with fear, the solution is to let go: to understand that, in reality, we've never needed the job.

The rest of the needs increase in difficulty. What would not needing approval or company be like? I have a friend who lives secluded in the countryside with his two dogs, rarely seeing anybody. He's happy living with nature and with the culture he accesses through the Internet. As we will see, maturity requires knowing how to be happy in complete solitude.

And we can continue to relinquish our needs to the extreme of letting go of life. In reality, it's not so hard to accept that life is fleeting and there's no obligation to live for a long time. Not fearing death is essential to avoiding hypochondria and coping well with the loss of loved ones, but also to living in the present with passion, as if there was no tomorrow.

But don't despair – in this book, we'll find all the mental strategies that we need to let go of all these attachments and become an apprentice of Christian martyrs, great travelers, and vibrant people like my friend Tina.

It's important to remember that fear stems from attachment, from an inability to let things go, while serenity and joy stem from detachment, from an absence of needs. We are going to learn to relinquish in a radical way, or in other words, become very strong on an emotional level.

Being happy in Cairo

I once had a patient of forty or so who owned a very successful wedding dress boutique. She was a loving and diligent wife and mother. Vanesa was great fun, so everyone liked her.

One day, we discussed the stress of being a mother. She had triplets, and aged twelve, they were a little "hyper." As she explained, "I'm at my wits' end. I never stop yelling. The kids are like a tornado. Nobody could cope with them. Just imagine, triplets!"

"All right, this is what we'll do: imagine you live in Cairo. That you're an explorer of ancient sites and you have a romance with a handsome photographer. At night, when you finish your day's work, you meet him at one of the city's rooftop restaurants," I suggested.

"Wow! Can he be like like Hugh Jackman?" she asked, laughing.

"Sure! Aside from your romance with Jackman, you have a fascinating job discovering ancient treasures. Try to imagine it: you live in an exotic country and have a fantastic life. Now, it's also true that Cairo is one of the most chaotic cities in the world, noisy and disorderly. But travelers love that – it's part of the magic of a city where anything is possible," I explained in detail.

"I see where you're going with this… you mean I could be as happy as an adventurer in a chaotic city like Cairo, but in my house, with the chaos of my kids," she replied.

"Exactly! See? You don't need peace and quiet to be happy. If you open your mind, you can enjoy the vitality of a city with traffic jams, noise, and strong smells all around. And likewise, you can be happy even with your children's lively disorder."

Over the course of the session, we looked at the arguments that showed Vanesa that she could experience bringing up her triplets in a different way without losing her serenity (later in the book, we see in more detail how we can desensitize ourselves to discomfort and chaos). Before long, she was able to peacefully read a novel while her children squabbled in the living room. In other words, my patient learned to happily let go of comfort, the third relinquishment in our pyramid of personal growth.

In another session I had with her, she asked, "Rafael, the work we're doing, does it mean no longer caring about anything? Giving everything up?"

"Yes. It's about finding the arguments to persuade yourself that no situation or adversity has to prevent you from being happy. Nothing: losing money, affection, comfort, peace itself or good health, even your life."

I should underline that, feeling calmer, Vanesa was able to implement what we call *the lesson of inner peace* with her children. That is, with patience and perseverance, she gradually taught them to behave in an "elegant" way so they would "become attractive boys, especially to the girls," as she put it. And they did!

However, for her mental well-being, it was essential that she stopped desperately needing her sons to be different from how they were. Not only that: in a broader sense, she learned to stop needing to be comfortable or peaceful, the other two relinquishments in our pyramid, never forget that strength is in letting go!

So far, we have seen two of the cornerstones of emotional change: looking inward and traveling light. Now, let's take a brief look at the third.

Step three: appreciating what's around you

In Buddhism – and in cognitive therapy – the art of appreciating your surroundings is fundamental. In Japan, they call it *wabi-sabi*. There are people who love life and others for whom the world seems boring, with little to offer. Both live in the same place. The difference is that some have turned on the light of appreciation, while others have turned it off; some are able to enjoy the little things, while others go in search of big emotions or nothing, and they tend to be left with nothing.

I remember a personal experience when I was very young that showed me what the practice of appreciation consists of and the results it offers. I was a psychology student, and aside from my studies, I organized concerts together with some friends. We did well and made good money from the activity.

One spring morning, I was walking through the campus with Jordi – my classmate and business partner – and my girlfriend at the time. I can't remember what we were chatting about, but at some point, Jordi said to my girlfriend, "What a life Rafael and I have! We're studying a subject we love, we organize amazing concerts, and we're loaded. This is what I call living!"

Happiness Declassified

My friend Jordi's words had a big impact on me. Simply because, until then, I hadn't stopped to consider the good life I had. I smiled. I looked around and contemplated the peaceful surroundings of the campus: the leafy trees, the sun's rays illuminating everything... and time slowed for a while. My mind was savoring the present.

This is the practice of appreciating life. The world is a place of abundance where extraordinary things never stop happening. And we're lucky enough to experience them because we're alive! We just have to stop and say it to ourselves, like Jordi did that morning.

It's wonderful to be able to see the colors of nature, breathe fresh air, listen to the harmonious sounds of music, and even feel the sensations of our own bodies! To a mind trained in appreciation, the world around is plentiful because there are endless things that are extraordinary. Then we're swimming in abundance, and the things that are supposedly lacking in our lives no longer matter. We're living in a *state of abundance.*

Wabi-sabi or appreciation can be for nature or for other beautiful things in the world or one's own life, as my friend Jordi did that spring morning. It's about going into an *appreciative mode*, which makes us feel good and is incompatible with complaining or *terribleitis*, the main instigator of neurosis.

This book will show us how to activate the art of appreciating what's around us. It is a daily practice that provides immediate emotional well-being and also heightens the two previous steps: looking inward and learning to travel light.

Making Every Day an Adventure

We have all had the experience of traveling abroad or to a new city. In these circumstances, almost all of us go into wabi-sabi mode. We walk around with our eyes wide open so that we take in all the beauty of the place; we take pictures that capture the present moment; we feel new, energetic, and in harmony. But in reality, that mental state is always inside us – not just when we're abroad – and if we experience it, it's because we're allowing ourselves to do so.

There's a lot of evidence that even mental states like those induced by drugs – such as ecstasy or Valium – can be reproduced at will if we know how, without needing to take anything. In reality, these states are caused by certain neuronal connections that follow a particular pattern. We can create these with drugs or with our thinking.

I have a friend who has learned to have multiple orgasms without ejaculating, using only mental techniques. His wife is thrilled! And so is he. His orgasms are very powerful, and with one after the other, he can continue to have sex in search of more emotions.

In the same way, we can all enter into wabi-sabi mode in our own city. There's no need to travel to be excited by the streets, the people, and the possibilities for enjoyment. Of course, to achieve this, we have to focus on beauty, do things a little more slowly, and stop from time to time to look and appreciate.

Falling in love with the first person that passes by

I often give lectures on love in which I express my conviction that anyone could fall in love with the first person who passes them by in the street. And I have proof to support this idea.

Anyone can choose someone at random and, within a short space of time, make them the person that they love, admire, and desire... because falling in love is a function of the mind, like laughing, or being in "fun" or joking mode – we can activate it or not activate it, and it depends more on ourselves than anything external.

I've studied abroad on two occasions: aged twenty in England and aged thirty in Italy. And in both places, I experienced a phenomenon that caught my attention. When we move to a different country – especially if we don't speak the language – we arrive in a completely new territory where we don't know anyone. It's true that we're full of excitement and energy, but we also go through a period of solitude because we're without our friends and family for a time.

The surprising thing is these experiences are incredibly fertile when it comes to forging great friendships and passionate romances. Within a few weeks, we make some great friends. Over the years, we create some unbreakable bonds. And the same thing happens in our love lives. Students often fall in love not long after arriving at university when, in their own city, they haven't met anyone special for years.

Why does this happen? Because people open themselves up. The first few weeks of solitude motivate us to make new bonds and *pam*! The magic happens. Couldn't we do the same thing at home?

If we appreciate what's around us, we fall in love with life. And it depends on us opening our minds, not on external things. As this book will show, this is one of the keys to emotional strength. We'll learn to do it every day. It will be like opening a third eye located in the middle of the forehead, in the prefrontal lobe, where our most beautiful thoughts and visions reside.

In this chapter we learned that:

Cognitive therapy can be summarised in three steps:

- Looking inwards: seeking wellbeing in our mental process, not in external circumstances.

- Learning to travel light: the ability to let go of anything that we lack or might lack. This makes internal threats and complaints disappear.

- Appreciating what's around us: an ongoing practice, appreciating the little things in life.

3
Being Happy in A Dump

A young doctor was at a psychiatric hospital. It was his first day at work. While he did his rounds, he came across a patient sitting in a chair, moving backwards and forwards, saying, "Lola, Lola, Lola!" over and over again.

"What's the matter with that man?" the doctor asked the head of the service.

"Oh, Lola! She was his unattainable love. He remembers her constantly," was his reply.

The young doctor continued to a padded cell where there was another patient banging his head against the wall, exclaiming, "Lola, Lola, Lola!"

Again he asked, "Is this patient's problem to do with the same Lola?"

"Exactly," the head replied. "But he's the man who married her."

This chapter is about letting go, the second step that we've already seen that I also call "learning to travel light." It is an essential step.

Every day that goes by, I am clearer that the success of therapy, of any personal growth, can be summarized as this: "Being happy in a dump." And clearer still that unhappiness is a consequence of the opposite, of what we might call "the stupid desire to stay in paradise".

If we grasp these two concepts, "being happy in a dump" versus "staying in paradise," we have made much of the change toward emotional strength and stability. After this moment of comprehension, our transformation will depend only on practice.

The Curious Post-Erasmus Low

In 1991, I was lucky enough to be an Erasmus student. I was accepted to a European student exchange program that had just begun. It was a wonderful year of my life. Just turned twenty-one, I travelled from Barcelona to the magnificent University of Reading in England.

We lived on an enormous campus, with student houses and halls of residence; there were people from all over the world, and lakes and beautiful fields...

In those early years of the Erasmus programme, nobody really knew what to do with the exchange students; most didn't even speak the host language! The lecturers looked at us with some sympathy and a little confusion. But as they say, "It's good fishing in troubled waters." I was delighted that we didn't have to take exams. It was a student paradise! Beautiful surroundings, a thousand experiences to have away from home, very little work, and a lot of beer.

The strange thing from a psychological point of view was experiencing a post-Erasmus low. That is, when the course ended and I returned to Spain, I was suddenly, unexpectedly overcome by a feeling of unhappiness and disorientation. And the curious thing is that I knew of many cases like mine: other students who felt depressed after that amazing year.

But why was I unhappy after such a great year? I should have been pleased to have completed my studies with a brilliant record, and I'd learned English and had some very enriching experiences. Plus, I had a fantastic life ahead of me! But the fact was, though I didn't understand why, I wasn't satisfied: I complained about my city, about my friends, about myself!

Only many years later did I understand what the problem was. It was due to none other than the fundamental cause of neurosis, depression, anxiety, anorexia, obsessions, jealousy... all human unhappiness!

Staying In Paradise

Humans have the unique capacity to compare. It's a great mental ability, but it also gives rise to a lot of problems.

We spend all our time comparing and evaluating: Is this restaurant going to be good? Yes or no... the answer depends on previous experiences. Do I like my job? That also depends on what I've experienced before!

For someone who has always eaten the same thing – a bland, boring meal – any restaurant would seem marvellous. And for someone who has been a slave in a coal mine, any decent job will seem like a cushy number.

Our different attitudes to things depend on the experiences we've had and the judgements we make based on those experiences. This is how we create our emotional state at any given time.

My post-Erasmus depression was due precisely to this: that year had been such a high, such an interesting and enjoyable time, that my mind told me that my life in Barcelona was a bore. And that it would continue to be unremittingly dull because what awaited me was nothing like my lost paradise: entering the world of work and giving up the student life, resuming a monotonous life in Spain in place of the excitement of living abroad, returning to my old friends instead of making lots of new ones.

My unhappy post-Erasmus experience lasted several years! It was mild compared to acute depression or any other neurosis that we psychologists and psychiatrists treat, but its structure was exactly the same.

Only years later did I figure out how it had happened and how I could have avoided it. And better still, I realised that I could reverse any exaggerated negative mental state with the same method: "avoiding attachment to paradises" in order "to be happy in a dump." That was the mental key to reversing my hang-ups.

Sure enough, emotionally vulnerable people are always trying to "stay in paradise." In other words, they believe that they will be well when they find a certain pleasant situation: if they find a partner like the one they had when they were young if they recover their social life, if they achieve a dream, or simply if they reach a good emotional state (which is nothing more than another "lost paradise").

And that's the root of the problem! Because lost paradises don't exist. Or, to put it differently, they are everywhere. Only by understanding this profoundly – or experiencing it! – can we find the philosopher's stone of strength?

Paradise Is Everywhere

Everything is relative. A Swiss landscape of green meadows and clear streams is stunning, but so are the barren lands of Castile, as the poets of Spain's Generation of 98 revealed. In their writing, Azorín and Unamuno described the bleak uplands, fallen trees, and bare rocks, and generations of Spaniards discovered that hidden beauty.

Two apparently contrasting scenarios can be equally as beautiful. How is that possible? It's very simple: because we humans invent those judgements. We believe that they are objective truths and refer to the intrinsic characteristics of things, but aside from whether our stomachs are empty or full – and little else –everything is invented, whether good or bad.

So when I told myself that life at the University of Reading was fantastic and that there was nothing to rival it, I believed that reality, without realising that I could have the same enjoyment I had in England in a Spanish prison as long as I opened my mind enough, as I had done at that university and as I now refused to do in Spain.

Being Happy in A Dump

So, the happiest and strongest people do just fine in a rubbish dump. And not only that: they've practised the right mental dialogue so much that they even *enjoy* feeling okay in situations that, on the surface, are adverse. There are two phenomena to consider here:

a) Human beings can ALWAYS create different perspectives in EVERY situation, making it interesting and enjoyable.
b) Mastering this art, which I call *reversing the emotion*, can become a pleasure in itself.

Not long ago, I had a patient, Arturo, who changed spectacularly with therapy. Once it was completed, he sent me the following email, which illustrates this love of being well in difficult situations:

> *This summer, I had a great experience that I want to share with you because I think it's a good example of much of what we learned in therapy. This August, I went on holiday alone for the first time in my life. The day I arrived on the mountain, I realised that I'd never been alone in the summer. As a child, I was with my parents, and since then, I have been with Laura, my wife. Of course, that was before she left me.*
>
> *When I arrived at my accommodation, I found that it was a dilapidated guesthouse – nothing like the photos and comments on the Internet. The room was tiny; it was on the main road, and there was quite a lot of noise well*

into the night. The décor was straight out of The Munsters.

I suppose I was unhappy because I'm used to good hotels – for work, I only stay in five-star establishments – and perhaps, it being my first solo holiday, I was sensitive, but the fact was it put me in a bad mood. I would say I even started to feel quite depressed.

But unlike what would have happened in my past life, my bad temper soon passed! I simply went for a walk around the village to persuade myself that I could be super happy there.

And do you know what, Rafael? Magic happened, as you often say! I convinced myself! In no time, I was happy to be in my room at the seedy guesthouse, beginning an unforgettable adventure.

But the best thing about these holidays (which have lasted a month!) is that I've had a lot of experiences like this. What you call "reversing the emotion". Every time I've felt unsettled – in a noisy restaurant when I had a flat tyre, one time I got lost in the mountain – I managed to transform it into peace and tranquillity.

What would have infuriated, depressed, or stressed me out before I no longer did? And I did it with my own mind! Again and again! As you well know, I was the kind of guy who was bothered by everything; my life was full of intolerable episodes, sad moments, and every other negative emotion that existed.

I have no words to express the happiness I feel now because I know for certain that the master of my emotional mind is me. And I love it!

"Being fine in a dump" means changing your mindset the moment you start to feel unsettled, making a huge, decisive effort to feel happy, regardless of the adversity in question. This is the key to emotional strength and freedom from hypersensitivity and neuroses.

The Practice of Reversing Our Emotions

As he explained to me in his email, Arturo was developing a knack for reversing his emotions using his determined new attitude. Every time he felt disturbed by something, he gave himself time to reason that there was nothing to complain about.

Indeed, the process of reversing a negative emotion is very satisfying because it's a bit like a miracle. At a given moment, you can be anxious, stressed, or scared… and in a very short space of time, you can be totally fine. For someone who has never experienced this personal power, it's mind-blowing.

But personal growth requires practice – a lot of practice – because, in most cases, it involves changing beliefs that we have clung to for years: "I can't be happy like this," "This is bad for me," "I can't stand this or that" …

A good practitioner of cognitive therapy would do well to practice reversing emotions every day. With this in mind, let's look at what kind of attitude it's good to have in the face of adversity and emotional crises.

A Matter of Suggestion

A man almost sixty years of age once came to see me with the following problem. He had recently started a relationship with a young woman under thirty, good-looking, cheerful and full of life.

Matías was a successful man, and he was happy to have found a woman who, as well as being beautiful, wanted to conquer the world, just as he felt one should live life. But now he was beset by a "terrible" problem: he couldn't get an erection with her. He explained to me, "It's not because I don't like her, Rafael. Because I promise you, she's hot. But something's wrong with me. I've tried Viagra, and not even that gets me hard. Can you believe it?"

"And if you masturbate alone, it works?" I asked.

"Nope. It's dead," he concluded, dejected.

Matías had been to see several urologists, and they'd done all kinds of tests without finding anything. But he couldn't get erections. And not only that, but his member had shrunk – it was smaller!

We assessed the issue, and he explained that the problem had begun just after they moved in together when the relationship started to get serious. Everything was fine until one night, disaster struck: his penis refused to stand tall. It hadn't worked again since then.

As we saw during his therapy, Matías's problem was purely a matter of suggestion. One fateful night, he couldn't get it up – nothing unusual for a man his age. But it scared him so much that, from then on, he "manufactured" psychological impotence for himself through the fear of being impotent itself.

Every day after that night, part of his brain had told him things like, "Oh God, don't let me be impotent!", "What will I do now?" or "Will she leave me?"

In many psychological conditions, there is an element of suggestion: we believe we're going to have a miserable time in certain situations (our 'dumps'), and in the end, it's what happens. Even the situation of being depressed or anxious. And that's what we experience! With the right mental programming, we can learn to tell ourselves that we *don't have a problem* and that we're going to discover that we're amazing people capable of being happy anywhere and in any situation.

Behavioural Work

In the therapy world, there is a school of *behavioural* therapy or *behaviourism*. It is often associated with the cognitive therapy that I practise in the form of what we call *cognitive behavioural therapy*. In behavioural psychology, the aim is to establish what it is that's disturbing the person and destroy the *object-feeling* association.

In fact, it's the same as the popular idea of facing one's fears in order to find out that they are just phantoms. In behavioural psychology, avoidance is the root of the problem because, in a way, it amplifies the feeling of dread. It's like when a person has a fall skiing down a slope and decides to give up skiing through fear. If, instead the fear is faced immediately, the fear-situation association may vanish.

The therapy that I practise has very little to do with behaviour and a lot to do with cognition. In other words, we focus on the thoughts that are behind emotions. We argue that such-and-such a situation doesn't have to unsettle you – being fine in a dump – and in this sense, it's not behavioural.

For instance, I gave up smoking when I persuaded myself that I didn't need cigarettes at all when I realised – deep down – that it brought me no pleasure: it was just a trick of the mind.

Nicotine is the most ingenious drug in nature because it creates an underlying anxiety in smokers and takes it away only when they smoke. Shortly after smoking, the nicotine increases the feeling of anxiety. The smoker's brain interprets the reduction in anxiety as pleasure but forgets that the cause of the anxiety in the first place was the cigarette itself. Once people know the truth about smoking – that is, that it's not a pleasure but a torture based on short withdrawals from the anxiety – they no longer have the desire to smoke. They no longer have to confront the problem; their logical mind has solved it.

So, we use cunning instead of strength, thinking rather than willpower. Our method is easy and doesn't involve "fighting" or gruelling effort.

However, we do have to work hard in order to change our emotional world, even if that work is exciting and fun. We have to expose ourselves to the "dump," but with the confidence that we can reverse it, and that the situation we fear can become a small paradise. And we do this with reasoning.

How Much Should I Expose Myself?

Many readers will be wondering right now up to what point they should expose themselves to this cognitive practice. When people have panic attacks, for instance, they suffer indescribable anxiety and find it almost impossible to face the situations in which an attack might overcome them. Or in the case of someone shy, they might have no desire to be among lots of people or interact…

My response is that we have to be generous with the exposure and get excited about reversing the negative emotion. I would say that once therapy – or our own personal work – has begun, it is useful to expose ourselves every day to the adversities that affect us at least once. During this exposure, we'll try to reason with ourselves about the best possible way to transform the disturbance. And, at the end of the day, we'll deserve a well-earned rest.

All in all, we have to work like someone going to the gym to build muscle. Some days, we'll achieve more than others, but we'll progress along the path to becoming an exceptionally strong and adaptable person.

Creating "Paradises"

Strong and happy people don't search for "paradises"; they create them! Or in other words, they transform "dumps" into "paradises." And how do they do it? By reasoning with themselves that they can be happy in any situation. With conviction and perseverance.

One of my patients once told me that what cognitive therapy suggested he should do was to try to "become a mixture of Mandela and Saint Francis of Assisi." Nelson Mandela because he was able to endure so many years unjustly imprisoned, and Saint Francis of Assisi because he was exultant, subjecting himself to all kinds of relinquishment (it's said that he slept on a large tombstone).

And yes! When he suggested this idea to me, I answered, "Well, the truth is that if you aspire to be like those people, you'll be very strong. They can feel great in any situation. If you open your mind to being fine in a "dump," how will you feel the rest of the time?"

The stoic philosophers called this phenomenon the "inner citadel," that is, possessing a character that creates well-being, regardless of external factors.

In this chapter we learned that:

- To be strong, you have to know how to create "paradises" in "dumps".
- Human beings can transform any situation into learning and pleasure. Our dialogue with ourselves is key in this process.
- Being unhappy, depressed or stressed has an element of suggestion and we can reverse negative emotions.
- The important thing when it comes to changing is understanding the situation from a different perspective, without fear of exposing ourselves.

4
The Cognitive Discussion

Little Red Cloud crouched to enter his grandmother's tent. She was beside the fire, washing tubers for their dinner. The smoke went out through the hole in the roof, so the inside was clean and warm.

The young Sioux seemed flustered. Grandmother asked him gently, "What's the matter, Cloud? You don't look good."

"It's my brother again! He went fishing with the others and left me on my own. He makes me so angry! Why are people so bad, Grandmother?"

"It's very simple, my child. Inside us all, there are two wolves: one is kind and happy, the other envious and mean. The two fight against each other inside us."

"And which one will end up winning?" the boy asked, his eyes wide.

"That's easy: the one you feed the most," the woman concluded.

I was walking one day in the mountains near Barcelona with my girlfriend, Claudia. It was a Sunday, and it was a beautiful day – the air was especially pure, so the invigorating smells of nature could be enjoyed in all their glory. The sky was bright, like a sheet of blue lacquer.

But that morning, before we started walking, something happened. While we had breakfast in a mountain café, the conversation turned to Ana, Claudia's best friend.

For some reason, Ana had it in for me. She didn't like me. And recently, on an outing I'd organised, she'd complained about everything the entire time. For her, the route was stupid; I didn't know how to guide them on the mountain, and, on top of that, according to her, I was an insufferable bossy-boots.

My argument with Claudia went more or less as follows:

"I don't want you to invite Ana on the excursions I organise," I said to her firmly.

"Rafael, Ana's lovely. And she does like you. It's just that sometimes she can be a pain in the neck. Let it go," she said in an affectionate tone.

"But she never organises anything and thinks she has the right to complain! If she arranged something once in a while, she'd realise how unpleasant it is to have someone stressing you out when you're trying to keep everyone happy," I said, raising my voice.

After talking about it for a while, we set off up into the mountain. But I was still annoyed because I hadn't managed to persuade Claudia to ban Ana from our outings. So I walked faster. I didn't feel like being beside Claudia. And at every bend, I infuriated myself even more with my thoughts: "Some girlfriend! She's not even on my side. There's no way I'm going to meet up with Ana again! She's a stupid cow!"

Happiness Declassified

Claudia, who is one of the sweetest people I know, puffed along behind me. She's loyal, loving, thoughtful, and incapable of hurting anyone, even if it harms her. But at that moment, that didn't stop my anger from building up inside my big, stubborn head. I was in a bad mood for an hour or so: I didn't speak, I had a long face, and I walked at an excessive pace by way of a punishment.

But perhaps thanks to the spirit of my favourite philosopher of ancient times, Epictetus, something in me changed. Still unsettled, I stopped to contemplate the tree-covered slopes from a mound, the beautiful colours, and I realised something: with my bad temper, I was only harming myself and the person I loved most.

I told myself, "Rafael, aren't you being a fool and ruining this wonderful Sunday over a silly little thing?"

I saw some vultures flying majestically overhead, silhouetted against the bright blue morning sky, and I became aware that I was wasting the moment. And every day that we live is a miracle that will never be repeated!

In this way, I managed to get my inner Epictetus to energetically insist, "Stop acting like a child! Turn around right now, say sorry to your girlfriend, and give her the kiss that she deserves!"

I turned and saw that Claudia was a long way back, panting. I took a step forward, but suddenly, another voice popped up in my mind. This time, it was the childish, irrational part of me. It said, "But Rafael, you can't change your mind now as if nothing's happened.

You're very angry! Ana's a moron, and Claudia's betraying you by defending her! You can't allow this behaviour; it's unbearable!" Of course, my neurotic mind was intent on arguing on the side of rage.

A gust of fresh air hit me in the face and reminded me again that the mountain was waiting for me, that I had all the nature and happiness in the world in front of me. So I said to myself, "That's enough nonsense!" And right there, I turned around to undo the stupid situation I'd created. Within a few minutes, after a few nice words, we were back on the trail again, brimming with happiness as we normally would be.

This story's not a big deal, but for some reason, it has stuck in my mind. I'm sure it's because it all happened so quickly: I reached a good level of rage in about forty minutes and managed to eliminate it in ten.

At any rate, the discussion I had with myself is an example of the work we do in cognitive therapy. Just as the philosopher Epictetus did in the first century, we transform ourselves through DISCUSSION with our own minds. Over and over, in an intensive, all-consuming way, until we change the way we think and feel.

The essence of the cognitive technique is to reverse negative emotions through dialogue with ourselves, gathering arguments until we see our difficulties in another light.

The aim is to change our negative emotions with our thoughts at the moment they arise. And if we do it well, we start to feel revitalised, experiencing an unusual sensation of well-being and belonging in the world. The aim is basically to persuade ourselves that the experience that's disturbing us doesn't have to do so: a long wait in the supermarket, our partner leaving us, physical pain, or anxiety itself.

The outcome of the discussion will always be something like this: "This won't prevent me from being happy; moreover, I'm going to have a fabulous day because I'm alive and I have a thousand opportunities to enjoy myself, regardless of what happens."

As we'll see below, although the idea is to persuade ourselves with arguments, it's not merely a question of positive thinking. It is essential that we acquire a new anti-complaining philosophy that is well grounded in reason.

The Two Stages of The Cognitive Discussion

The cognitive discussion has two stages:

a) Determine the attachment: what we believe is so important.

b) Let go of it: remove all its absurd significance.

Let's see an example. Marcos was a fifty-something director of an insurance company. He came to see me because he was permanently tense and suffered from insomnia. Work was making him so stressed that, for the past year, every Sunday, he had an anxiety attack because of how much he dreaded the arrival of Monday.

The first thing he learned in therapy was to detect how he caused the stress in himself. Almost without realising it, he would say, "I

HAVE TO BE a totally capable worker. In life, ONE MUST do things absolutely right, at least when it comes to work. If they fired me from the company, I'd be a terrible FAILURE as a person, and my life would be a complete DISASTER". These sentences summarised his hyper-pressurising ideology in relation to work, though he wasn't even aware that he demanded so much of himself.

What was Marcos attaching himself to? To his work, to his image as an effective person, and to status. With the right argumentation – which we'll look at in detail in the coming chapters – Marcos learned to mentally let go of everything he considered so important. The second stage of his cognitive work, therefore, was to let go.

Letting Go

When we let go, we can be happy in spite of adversity. Yes, human beings can enjoy life regardless of their difficulties because they are nothing more than threats fabricated by unnecessary attachments. If using logic, we can accept the possibility of losing this or that, magic happens! We don't really care about our feared situations anymore.

My patient Marcos learned to mentally let go of everything to do with work. He realised that no one has to be efficient or needs to work. All we need is to love life and others. He saw that if he was fired, he could be happy in many other ways. In fact, he wouldn't die of hunger because his wife would be more than happy to support him if it meant he was no longer so unhappy, and he would be able to devote himself to his passions: Egyptology and teaching.

Letting go is a mental exercise that enables us to remove the excessive importance that we attach to everything. Paradoxically, once we do it, everything becomes much more manageable – we begin to enjoy our tasks and have more success.

To let go, we must gather all the evidence that we need to persuade ourselves that we need very little in life in order to be happy. This might take the form of a healthy comparison: "Are there other people who have never possessed what I'm afraid of losing and, in spite of everything, are happy?"

There is also the technique of the *valuable action question*: "To what extent does this – or would this – difficulty prevent me from doing valuable things for myself and others?"

The answers to these questions are YES, there are people who're happy with very little, and YES, there are ALWAYS valuable things to do that can fulfil us.

In cognitive therapy, we use every possible argument to persuade ourselves that there is NEVER any need to "worry" because we understand that the emotion is stupid and paralysing. It's much more useful to always be cheerful, to activate our enjoyment, and to pursue our goals without a hint of fear.

It's okay to feel a little upset with someone like Ana, who had it in for me, or perhaps felt jealous that Claudia was my girlfriend. But we'll get over it much more quickly if we don't make a big deal out of it.

It's useful to want to do our work as well as possible, but it's absurd to place as much pressure on ourselves as Marcos did, to the point that he was unable to sleep at night.

And the only way to *occupy* ourselves rather than *preoccupy* ourselves is to let go. The idea is to tell ourselves, "Well, if it doesn't happen, it won't be the end of the world."

THE COGNITIVE DISCUSSION		
ADVERSITY	STAGE 1: Determine the attachment	STAGE 2: Let go of it
I'm stressed at work.	If I'm fired, I'll be a total FAILURE.	I don't need a job to be happy.
	As a person, I MUST do my work perfectly.	The most important quality isn't efficiency but one's capacity to love.
	My family and friends think I'm USELESS.	If those around me think that, it's because they have the wrong value system. The problem is theirs, not mine.

From Bad to Good, In Twenty Minutes

In the discussion technique, another important element is to seek to transform the emotion: reverse the negative feeling in the moment and feel great instead.

A transformation experience like this is very powerful because we humans believe in the power of negative emotions – we see them as being more solid than they really are! We're fooled by them. For instance, if your partner leaves you and you get depressed, you believe that the depression is real and that it will be hard to get over. However, it doesn't have to be like that. At my practice, on countless occasions, I've witnessed how an "abandoned" person can stop being unhappy in a single session – forever! They arrive in a bad state and leave feeling elated to be alive, and the problem ends there.

If we want to transform ourselves into strong, happy people in all areas of life, we have to develop the ability to reverse a negative emotion at any given time. And it can be done!

We might not manage to transform the emotion every time, but we always have to try. If we don't manage it, bad luck, but the next day, we have to try again. With this discipline, we'll gradually shape a new, stronger, happier mind.

Banishing Terribleitis

Before finishing this chapter and moving on to a practising cognitive discussion with examples of the most typical neuroses, let's define a term that I'll use throughout the book: *terribleitis* or *catastrophising*.

When my patients complain too much about their difficulties, I usually tell them they have terribleitis, that they're catastrophising. When we catastrophise, we tell ourselves, "This is unbearable, terrible, I can't stand it," and it's this inner dialogue that generates exaggerated negative emotions.

With cognitive discussion, we *decatastrophise* – we learn to see any problem as a minor detail, just as Mandela or Saint Francis would… Because we want to be like them, right?

In this chapter we learned that:

- The cognitive technique consists of changing our internal dialogue, minimising the importance of the exaggerated negative thoughts that we have.
- Cognitive discussion has two stages:

a) Identifying the attachment: noticing what it is exactly that we're telling ourselves to make ourselves feel depressed – it's always an "asset" that we don't want to lose.

a) Letting go: understanding that we've never needed the asset in order to be happy.

- The cognitive method is about using arguments to persuade ourselves – it's not just a question of positive thinking.

Part Two:
Grasping the Methodology
5
Models of Emotional Strength

A young man named Sira joined a monastery where the monks lived in strict silence. Every five years, the brothers spoke their minds to the abbot but were only permitted to say two words.

At the end of the first long five-year period, Sira was called before the old man.

"Anything to say?" his superior asked.

"Hard bed," the young man replied.

Another five years went by, and the scene was repeated. The abbot asked:

"Anything to say?"

"Terrible food!" Sira exclaimed. And after another five years:

"Anything to say?"

"Bathroom stinks."

After another five-year period, twenty now have passed:

"Anything to say?"

"I'm leaving!" the monk replied.

"Thank goodness! Because since you've been here, you've done nothing but complain!" the wise abbot concluded.

We human beings are bound to one another. So far, science hasn't expressed an opinion – maybe it's hormones that we give off or magnetic fields that we emit – but the truth is that nothing is more powerful to us than a fellow human. Countless people have been emotionally struck by others, stirred, and influenced. For example, many young people, after witnessing the brilliant work of an artist, decide to devote their lives to their art.

Jesus Christ, Buddha, and Lao-Tzu were role models who changed the course of humanity. And for many years, my role model has been the wheelchair-bound British scientist Stephen Hawking. How many times do my meditations feature him? Since a few years ago, very early in the morning, I always swim-meditate for half an hour. As I swim, I often wonder, "What would Stephen Hawking think of this or that?" Through his perspective, all my worries fade away.

I consider this chapter essential. It describes some mega-models of emotional strength. Let no one be in any doubt that, reading about them, rays of their wisdom will penetrate some part of our brain until they lodge themselves in our emotional mind.

Learning from a youngster

A patient named Rubén came to me and said, "I'm depressed." He was forty-three years old, and what he meant by that statement was that he had always been sad and lacked the ability to enjoy things. He also admitted that he tended to worry too much about everything. Just then, for instance, his girlfriend wanted to sell her home, and it caused him a lot of stress. I asked why, and he listed a whole series of potential pitfalls: not getting a good price, not finding a new property they liked, and being overwhelmed by the move.

Rubén was going through a patch in which his depression and anxiety had spiraled, and in reality, it was his girlfriend who had pushed him into coming to my practice. He didn't have much belief that he could change. He looked at me with suspicion and adopted a very passive attitude. I realized that he needed to know that change is possible! Otherwise, he would never open his mind or put any effort into the therapy. So I decided to tell him about Daniel Stix.

I read about Daniel in the Spanish current affairs magazine *XL Semanal*. It was an interview to promote his book *Con ruedas y a lo Loco* (*On Wheels Like There's No Tomorrow*). In the photos, he was handsome and healthy, a blossoming seventeen-year-old. But, as the title of his book hinted, a wheelchair went everywhere with him. Daniel was born with cancer. He had a large lump on his back, and the doctors decided to operate and treat him with chemotherapy. Eight days after he was born, he underwent his first treatment. Some start in life! At the end of the treatment, a kidney had to be removed, but against all odds, he survived, though he was left paralyzed.

This young man from Madrid, a Paralympic champion in various sports, told the journalist, "I don't feel different. Sure, I am paraplegic. I was born with cancer. My parents, like many other people, didn't know that a baby could be born with cancer. The likelihood of having a congenital neuroblastoma is very small, and the doctors didn't give me much chance of surviving. But I did, and I guess in that sense, I've been lucky. But in everything else, I'm a normal person – with my whole life ahead of me!"

I showed Rubén the two photos that appeared in the article: one showed Daniel in the national basketball team vest waving to the crowd, and the other showed him as a five-year-old boy in a little wheelchair. I said to Rubén, "Daniel Stix is positive and strong, like many people with disabilities I've met. You, my friend, are in good health, and yet you are not. This sixteen-year-old boy, with his bomb-proof inner dialogue, has a lot to teach us, don't you think?"

Rubén studied the pictures for a few long seconds. He seemed to get the message, but then, he shook his head and blurted out, "But this kid's right in the head. And I'm not! My illness is much worse! There's nothing harder than being like me."

"You're wrong," I snapped back. "If you're 'not right in the head,' it's because you've spent your whole life moaning about real and future adversities. And if he's mentally strong, it's because he decided, as a child, that we would never complain. You can change! He's strong because he decided to be and through constantly working on his mind.

Then I pointed out another paragraph from Daniel's interview in which he said, "I've never thought of being in a wheelchair as adversity, though I know that in a lot of things, I have to work harder than everyone else. Overall, I think I've been very lucky. I'm very grateful for all the opportunities that have come my way."

Rubén read it and fell silent. I could almost see his mind working. He was starting to move in the right direction, the opposite of his usual way of thinking. I went on. "And look what he says here: 'It's about adopting the right mentality. There are people who end up in a wheelchair, and they become bitter. But if you see the light, you realize that happiness doesn't depend on whether you're crippled or not.'."

Young Daniel Stix was giving us the key. Cognitive psychology teaches us precisely this: that everything is in our heads, and emotional strength can be acquired; it's about developing the right mindset. My patient could do it, too.

In the following sessions with Rubén, we discussed his fears. We looked at how he talked about them and also what young Daniel would say to himself. For example, we examined the issue with his girlfriend's home. I placed him in the worst-case scenario, a very useful de-catastrophizing technique.

"What's the worst thing that could happen with the sale of the house?"

"The worst?" he said with a wry smile. "Well, girlfriend could be left homeless!"

"And if that happens, will she die of thirst, starve, freeze to death?" I asked.

"Well, no," he said, half laughing. "She would come and live with me, but we would be very cramped in my apartment."

"Rubén, answer me this: What does being cramped have to do with happiness? Let me read you this from Daniel Stix: 'My favorite holidays are on the beach. My chair doesn't work there, but I've learned to drag myself along. I can injure myself on the sand in the water, so I wear a wetsuit. For me, obstacles are challenges, and I always manage to overcome them and have a good time.'."

Rubén was beginning to understand. His problem with depression was reduced to a succession of complaints, or "terribleitis." And now he was beginning to adopt "the right mentality," as Daniel Stix put it. If he could change his beliefs about each adversity, his overwhelming negative emotions would disappear forever.

Being exceptional

The people I'm going to describe in this chapter are all exceptional, like Daniel Stix, and it's very important to realize that we can all be like them. Cognitive therapy goes beyond healing neuroses stopping depression, jealousy, and worrying. Our goal is much more ambitious: we aspire to be people like Daniel Stix, Ana Amalia, and Lary León, the next two examples. We want to – and we can – become entities in the world with a special energy capable of turning any situation into an exciting life adventure. We all have the choice to live every minute with passion, joy, and the ability to "reinvent" ourselves.

I once had a fantastic patient who underwent in-depth cognitive therapy. As a result, she experienced a radical change. Montserrat went from being admitted for several months each year to hospital units for depression and anxiety to being the strongest and happiest person in her family. With huge creativity, she explained to me that she had developed a kind of meditation that she called "microvisualisations," which consisted of concentrating continually, for every hour of the day, on doing everything rationally, enjoying herself, and banishing any complaining from her mind. With this work, Montserrat had become an exceptional person. Her whole family was surprised by her transformation. In fact, when they had problems, they went to her.

As we will see in the examples below, what defined her personality now was her determination to live passionately at all times, whatever happened.

Simply reinventing yourself

Another of my role models in recent years has been Ana Amalia Barbosa, a 49-year-old Brazilian woman who became tetraplegic after suffering a stroke at the age of 35. I learned about her through an interview in the Spanish newspaper *El Mundo*. Ana Amalia is unable to move any part of her body except for some muscles in her face. Nor can she speak or swallow. However, she leads an exciting life devoted to teaching children with cerebral palsy and researching the field.

Happiness Declassified

Ana Amalia communicates with the world by blinking and indicating letters of the alphabet. And in this way, she writes books! She also paints using a computer program that captures the movements of her chin.

I found some photos of her on the internet: she has short, dark hair and always wears a faint smile. She is 5 feet 2 inches tall and confined to a wheelchair that looks enormous. Ana Amalia is very well known in Brazil because, despite her immobility, she does great work with children with cerebral palsy. She received a doctorate cum laude from the University of São Paulo, one of Latin America's most prestigious institutions. Ana Amalia also writes books about her life experiences. Of course, she always does so with the help of her assistants, who translate her blinking and signals into words.

Ana Amalia needs assistance for much of her work, but she has no shortage of helpers. Every day, a teacher helps her give lessons to the children with PowerPoint presentations. In another interview I found online, her young assistant said through tears that working with Ana Amalia was the best thing that had happened in her life because her boss was teaching her, quite literally, to live big.

In the *El Mundo* interview, when Ana Amalia was asked to describe her life after her stroke, she answered with one word: "Reinvention." She didn't say "hard work" or even "adaptation" but chose a much more positive word: she saw her situation as an opportunity to learn to do new things, to reach people in a more profound way, to be reborn in a different skin.

In recent times, Ana Amalia has helped me with many patients. When they arrive in an especially low mood, I show them the *El Mundo* interview and ask them, "What would this woman tell you about your situation? Do you have any reason to complain?"

The journalist who interviewed Ana Amalia noticed that she had a large card hanging from her with the alphabet printed on it so that her assistant – or anyone else – could decipher her blinking when she spelled out words. One wonderful detail was that Ana Amalia had had cards of different colors made for her so they would match her clothes each day. According to her mother, Ana Amalia was very vain and had continued to be after the stroke.

Strength, the joy of living, energy, beauty: all of this is within our reach – in any situation – if we focus in the right way, decisively.

Cognitive therapy teaches us to never complain. The strongest and happiest people never lament their situation because they truly believe there is nothing that's so bad that it will prevent them from being happy. Ana Amalia is proof of this. But we often insist on seeing our adversity as something intolerable: our partner has left us, and we're unemployed... what is all that compared to Ana Amalia's extreme paralysis? There's no real reason to complain in this world! Let's enjoy life now! Among Ana Amalia's disabilities is the fact that she can't chew or swallow, so she is fed special purées that are injected into her stomach. But her real nourishment has nothing to do with food. She draws her life force from her rational way of thinking. And life is full of opportunities for those who stop complaining and open themselves up to life's most beautiful possibilities.

A real-life mermaid

Perhaps the principle that best sums up the philosophy of cognitive psychology is this: "We can be happy in any situation" – whether we're in prison, waiting to be operated on in a hospital, or suffering from chronic anxiety. It's all in our heads! And we should be glad because this is a certainty. If something disturbs us at any time in our lives, it is only because we believe that the situation is "very" difficult, and we create a mental picture that makes us experience it this way.

In my talks, I often mention great travelers because they are able to enjoy themselves in practically any situation. For them, complex circumstances are never overwhelming; they are always vibrant moments of discovery.

We can all learn to be like this with each of our adversities. Let's erase from our minds the absurd belief that we can't be okay here or there, this way or that!

Let's make the magic happen!

Lary León is a beautiful journalist who works at the Spanish TV channel Antena 3. She's in her mid-thirties and has just written a book about her life entitled *Lary, el tesón de una sirena* (Lary, the Tenacity of a Mermaid). Lary was born in Guadalajara with incomplete arms (as if they had been amputated at the forearm) and only one leg, but she was and is a "complete" person in every sense. More than complete: she's a beacon of joy and vitality for the people around her.

When she talks about herself, Lary explains that as a child, she believed she was a little mermaid because she had fins (for arms) and a long and beautiful tail (her one leg). And the best thing is that she still thinks she is, albeit metaphorically, a magical being who is in this world to help awaken others.

Lary is an exceptional person because she has learned that happiness depends on what we do with what we have, not on our situation itself. In a television interview, she said, "I discovered a long time ago that I have a mission in life, and that is to show by example that we can all love and enjoy life."

Let's open our ears wide!

She added, "Any disability is an opportunity to develop a superpower which, in many cases, exceeds all the expectations we had about ourselves."

In other words, adversity is an opportunity to develop other, more refined, and beautiful ways of enjoying life. Chapter 14 explains how depression is not a disadvantage and that any adversity, even depression, can be a path to virtue. And that virtue – loving others, being kind and honest – can lead us to the Fourth Dimension of Existence! Everything – even pain – can be transformed into enjoyment if we know how to seize the moment and develop a superpower. Then, we will all be mermaids and supermen. Real ones.

The three models of emotional strength that we've seen – Daniel Stix, Ana Amalia Barbosa, and Lary León – are just a few of the hundreds of thousands who exist in the world. For whatever reason, they have received media attention, but the other 99% live among us in anonymity.

Whenever an emotion disturbs us, we can look to them and strengthen our commitment to our therapy and to building mental strength. From that moment on, we will stand alongside those who work fearlessly every day to improve their emotional resilience.

A carousel of role models

A very advanced patient once told me about a meditative technique he had developed. It consisted of reflecting on the following: "What would my models of emotional strength tell me about my possibilities in life?" And then I imagined Stephen Hawking, Christopher Reeve (aka Superman), Albert Casals... – and all those I've described in my books – on a carousel of short videos, one after the other. My patient performed this exercise whenever he was tempted to complain about something and also as a daily meditation.

Let's look back at some of the role models I've described in my books:

   • Stephen Hawking, the wheelchair-bound scientist who has been unable to move or speak for forty years.

• Thomas Buergenthal, a judge of the International Court of Justice in The Hague, survived a Nazi extermination camp as a child and decided to be happy.

• Nick Vujicic, the young man with no arms or legs, gives inspirational talks and always finishes by hugging each participant.

• Albert Casals is a boy in a wheelchair who has been traveling the world without money since the age of fifteen.

• Jean-Dominique Bauby, the journalist who, like Ana Amalia, was left tetraplegic and who wrote the beautiful best-seller *The Diving Bell and the Butterfly*.

If we had them in front of us, they would offer us a radically positive outlook on life! They would say something like, "Kid, you have nothing to complain about! Whatever your problems are, life is waiting for you to seize it. Forget those minor details and enjoy yourself!"

The carousel of role models is a wonderful tool that I have adopted in my own daily emotional workout, and I can confirm that it works. How could it not, with such fine teachers?

In this chapter we learned that:

- Mental workouts help us to be emotionally strong.
- Models of strength tell us that the secret is in our inner dialogue. They were not born with this wisdom, so we can all increase our emotional resilience.
- The model carousel is a tool we can use to visualise several models of strength, reminding ourselves what they would do in our place.

6
Tuning in To Harmony

A young man went to a logging camp to ask for work. The foreman, seeing that he was strong, employed him without a second thought. He could start the next day.

On his first day on the mountain, he worked hard and felled dozens of trees.

On the second day, he worked just as hard, but he was only half as productive.

On the third day, he was determined to improve. He swung his axe furiously all day. Even so, the result was much worse.

When the foreman noticed the young man's lack of progress, he asked, "When was the last time you sharpened your axe?"

And the young man replied, "I haven't had time. I've been too busy felling trees!"

In this chapter, we will discuss one of the fundamental – and also one of the most beautiful – tools of cognitive psychology. I call it tuning into harmony, and it consists of making an effort to appreciate the things around us. This is the third pillar of cognitive psychology, as we saw in Chapter 2. Let's remember the three steps to gaining emotional strength:

1. Looking inwards
2. Learning to walk lightly

74

3. Appreciating the things around us (or tuning in to harmony)

We're going to examine this skill in detail and learn to use it to boost our emotional strength.

Josefina, light in the darkness

Many years ago, when I started practicing as a psychologist, I worked with an association for people with a chronic illness. More specifically, women because Sjögren's syndrome most commonly affects older females. My job was to provide group therapy for sufferers. Sjögren's syndrome causes extreme dryness in all the mucous membranes – mouth, eyes, skin –, severe muscular pain, and terrible fatigue, and so far, there is no cure. Many women with Sjögren's develop depression.

Every week, I sat with a group of eight to ten women aged fifty to sixty around a big table, and we discussed mental strategies for being happy in adversity. Some of the women were positive and cheerful, and others were the opposite: professional moaners.

But I will never forget Josefina, who was a gem. She wore dark glasses to ward off eye pain and always wore a wide smile. Her symptoms were among the most acute, and yet she was a shining light for the other women – she was always radiant.

In our group talks, Josefina would say very valuable things:

"I go out every morning to see the sunrise, although the Sjögren makes my eyes very sensitive. I walk on the beach and, often, I stop in front of the sea and cry with joy."

In every meeting, this little woman gave us a lesson in positive psychology. She told us how she "tuned in her mind" every day to appreciate the beauty of life and thanked God for what she saw: the colors, the movements of the sea, the blue sky. And she attributed her emotional well-being to this personal effort. Every day, Josefina lit herself up.

We can all learn to "light ourselves up" or tune into harmony; in other words, practice exercises to contemplate and appreciate the surroundings that have a positive effect on us:

- They calm us down.
- They increase our serotonin and dopamine levels.
- They bring us joy.
- They dispel our fears and neuroses.
- They help us to understand the cognitive principles of mental health.

Opening the mind

I love history, and on occasion, I've read that, like Josefina, mystics performed exercises to "light themselves up." As we will see, there isn't much difference between tuning into God or into nature or the world's beauty. In around 1550, Teresa of Ávila, the famous Spanish mystic, wrote:

Oh, beauty that surpasses!
Oh, beauty that surpasses all beauties!
Without wounding, You hurt, and without hurting, You undo the love
of creatures.

Oh, knot that binds two things so unequal, I know not why you come untied, for when you are bound you give the strength

to accept one's ills as good. You bind those who have no being with the Being unending; without ending, you end,

without having to love, you love, you exalt our nothingness.

In this poem, Saint Teresa describes the open mind of someone who is in complete harmony with themselves and with the world. To the point, as she says in such a poetic way, of "accepting one's ills as good"; in other words, being happy despite our adversities.

Experiential learning

But what specifically does the exercise of *tuning into harmony, lighting ourselves up,* or *appreciating our surroundings* consist of? We could define it as a practice that cultivates a non-catastrophizing frame of mind but through experience rather than through cognition and rational arguments.

By practicing harmony, we experience happiness in the present moment for no specific reason. We just want to enjoy the present. And this exercise of enjoying the little things means that we need very little in order to be okay, and this is one of the principles of this therapy.

Some ways to experience this attunement are:

- Strolling through the city contemplating its beauty: architecture, lighting, etc.
- Walking through nature with the same contemplative mindset.
- Listening to music and delighting in it.
- Taking pleasure from nice thoughts.

- Enjoying the moment while you work: trying to do it well and elegantly.
- Having a nice conversation and appreciating it.
- Enjoying personal virtues: being kind to others, well organized, honest
- Enjoying art.

Tuning in involves practicing one of these activities every day and noticing the pleasure they bring, making a commitment to orientating yourself towards enjoyment, and eradicating catastrophizing, necessitaties, and complaining.

Good attunement walks

Cognitive psychology teaches us that emotional states are like musical channels that we tune into. We are often stuck on negative channels, but we can turn over and tune into good-vibe channels into harmonious ones. I have been a hiker for a long time, and it's one of the most de-stressing activities I know of. After walking for hours through nature, for no purpose except to go from one place to another, I feel almost completely relaxed. No matter how agitated we are, being in good company, the colors and sounds of nature, and the leisurely exercise pacify us.

When we're stressed, jumpy, fearful, or neurotic, it's because we're stuck on the wrong channel. It's the channel of struggling, "duty," and complaining. At this point, our task is to tune into another channel, and finding the poetry around us helps us do this. And it's always there!

With this in mind, my patients learn to go for attunement walks. Making the most of the de-stressing effects of walking, they stroll around the city admiring the beautiful buildings and the gigantic trees, enjoying the breeze, and listening to music on their headphones.

The poem below by Juan Ramón Jiménez must have been the result of one of these harmonious walks. In it, he sings in rapture to a poplar, a surprising tree that seems to be bathed in silver. (In Madrid, there is a majestic specimen in the botanical garden next to the Prado Museum.)

TO THE SILVER POPLAR

The bird sings above, and the water sings below (Above and below, my soul opens up.)

Between two melodies, the silver column. Leaf, bird, star; low flower, root, water. Between two riots, the Silver Column. (And you, ideal trunk, between my soul and my soul.)

The trill rocks the star, the wave the low flower. (Above and below, my soul trembles.)

The more we tune into channels of harmony, the more our minds heal. The more days we spend tuning in, the better we feel. Step by step, this pacifying work will do its job.

A daily pill

Many years ago, I met a person who told me about attunement walks, and now, writing these lines, I remember him. I had just finished university, and I was working temporarily at a human resources factory. The place was in a remote area of Zaragoza province, on the outskirts of a town named Mequinenza. The factory was surrounded by fields and hills, and there was a vast lake.

One day in August, during the lunch break, Tomás and I started chatting. He was about fifty years old, with a few surplus kilos and a tanned complexion. He worked as an engineer in charge of the factory machines and always – always – exuded tranquillity and happiness. We were discussing stress and mental health in a large company like ours, and he said, "For many years, before starting work, I've gone walking in the fields. I look at the crops, see how they are and how they're growing; I breathe the fresh air and recharge my batteries."

"How long do you spend walking?" I asked.

"At least half an hour. But nearly always an hour."

Not by chance, Tomás seemed to be the happiest guy in the company.

The miracle of the little things

Another way to experience the wonder of life and see that we need very little to be happy is to perfect our ability to appreciate the small things. It's what I called the practice of *wabi-sabi* in chapter 2. It could be said that emotional strength and happiness are found in the little things in life: a glass of wine, a well-written article, a nap after lunch, a burst of fresh air in the morning... When patients are very anxious or depressed – demoralized, perhaps – I often ask them to spend a lot of time appreciating the little things: drink a glass of good wine, stroll around a pleasant area, treat themselves to small pleasures, and try to savor them intensely, like the miracles that they are. As soon as they start, they free themselves a little from the tombstone they have on top of them.

Have you ever wondered why Christians pray before meals? It's a very rational exercise! They give thanks for basic things like food in order to appreciate them, to experience them intensely, to make them pillars of our happiness. But the strongest and happiest people I have met are grateful not just for their lunch but also for the most everyday things that tend to go unnoticed, like the fact that there is air in the atmosphere, light, or color!

A great friend of mine, a Catholic nun, once said to me, "Do you realize how lucky we are to be alive and to able to appreciate the light?"

"Yes!" I noted. This very moment is precious because sometime in the future – near or distant – humanity and the Earth will cease to exist.

In Japan, there is a literary tradition that alludes to this appreciation of the small things: the haiku, short poems that extol the wonders of our surroundings. They don't have to rhyme, and they portray tiny details experienced as beautiful miracles.

Here is a haiku by the Buddhist monk Onitsura, composed in the seventeenth century:

Come here, come here!

I cry, but the fireflies

just fly away.

Or, from the same time, another by the monk Buson:

He short night:

bubbles of crab froth

among the river reeds.

And one last haiku from the famous poetess Tatsuko:

White are the faces that observe

the rainbow.

There are few things as therapeutic as composing a little poem each day. Because *wabi-sabi* – appreciating the small things – is an act that embodies all the wisdom of cognitive psychology.

Post-its on the wall

There's a word I expelled from my vocabulary a long time ago: "despachar." In Spain, we use this word to mean "to deal with something" in order to move on to something else, but the problem is that this approach is how human beings stupidly let life pass us by because we don't savor it. Doing things mechanically sends us on a mindless race to nowhere. The wonderful game of life takes place in the present moment.

Happiness Declassified

Our enormous capacity to enjoy ourselves lies in the here and now, in everyday tasks, and in our ability to appreciate and approach everything with passion. But we often forget this. The human mind, especially in big cities, tends to race for the absurd reason that everyone is doing it. Without realizing it, we join a mad dash. We start doing things thinking, "Let's see if I can finish all this quickly so I can have a good time later." But then we're so worn out, agitated, or fed up that we're no longer in the right frame of mind to enjoy ourselves.

To avoid wasting life by always being in a hurry, we can use reminder tools. The Buddhist monk Thich Nhat Hanh was the founder of a well-known monastery in the south of France named Plum Village. This Vietnamese monk, poet, and peace activist brought a large bell from his native country that can be heard anywhere on the site. At unexpected times of the day – more or less every half an hour – someone takes their turn to ring it. It is a beautiful but penetrating *gong* that takes a few long seconds to fade – *goooong!* – and everyone knows that it's time to stop, breathe in, breathe out, and say to themselves: "I hear the bell. This wonderful sound brings me back to my true home." The monastery cook puts down his knives for a moment, the administrator looks away from the computer, the teacher falls silent, and the students stop listening. At that moment, everyone renewed their commitment to performing their tasks with love and intensity.

At my Barcelona practice, I have a custom similar to that of the Plum Village gong. On the walls, on my computer, and on my desk, I stick Post-its with reminders: "Focus on your patient!", "Enjoyment is here, now!", "This very task is the most glorious!" "No *despachar*!", "Be happy now!"...

All these notes remind me that my big moment is the present: at midday, in front of the computer, writing an article. Or at five in the afternoon, just before receiving a patient. Or at lunchtime, while I savor a delicious wine! In each and every one of those moments, I commit to working with as much enjoyment, attention, and passion as possible. Not later! Now!

Exercises of paying attention to the present are very useful when it comes to tuning into harmony, and it is no coincidence that they are important practices in all spiritual traditions. Christian monks stop working seven times a day to pray or meditate and focus on the essential, which is none other than happiness itself.

total commitment to joy

As a child, I was educated at the Salesians of Horta, and there, every day, we performed a rather healthy ritual: first thing, before going into the classroom, we gathered in the playground and sang a religious song: ***Alegre la mañana que me habla de ti*** ("Joyful the morning that tells me about you"). The song was fitting of those splendid Mediterranean mornings in Barcelona: bright light, blue sky, and aromas of the surrounding countryside.

It was like a personal manifesto with which we pledged to live life enjoying ourselves and appreciating our surroundings. Not bad at all!

And in adulthood, any day we feel like it, we can compose our own manifesto in defense of happiness. It goes something like this:

A MANIFESTO FOR HAPPINESS

Today and for the rest of my days, I pledge to live with passion, to appreciate my surroundings, and to value the little things.

I shall banish complaints from my mind because they serve no purpose.

I shall forget about what I lack and focus on what I possess and my future opportunities.

I redouble my commitment today to loving my environment, working carefully, doing all I can, and thanking nature for its gifts.

I will live with poetry.

I will put absurd needs aside. I will find beauty in everything.

I will treat myself and others with loving care.

Every day, love, passion, acknowledgment, and beauty will flood my mind and all my actions.

A commitment to beauty

Entering the realms of rationality, we become aware that life is beautiful and that we human beings have an enormous capacity to appreciate it.

When we reach a profound level of emotional well-being, we can be enraptured by the brightness of the sun's rays on a spring morning, the rectangular shapes of a beautiful building, someone's kind gesture on the street... At this point, you feel great in your own skin and in the world.

People who are often in this state of enrapture tend to try to create beauty around them. It is of the kind that architects of old imbued their projects with. The kind that the educator Maria Montessori sought when she founded her rational schools. The kind that artisans use in their creations. Visionaries drink in beauty and feel compelled to produce more beauty in a cycle like rainfall and evaporation from the sea. This commitment to beauty makes our rationality reverberate; it drives it, augments it, and fixes it in our minds. If all the architects in the world had this commitment, the world would be a better place. If all teachers, police officers, and psychologists did so, there would be far less neurosis and much more joy and fulfillment.

This attitude is one of the aspects of cognitive therapy that must be practiced, cultivated, and renewed so that it permeates everything we do. It shows in our appearance and our way of relating to others. It requires commitment, but it's a very pleasant endeavor! A commitment to beauty also helps us stop worrying.

A good friend, an entrepreneur and practitioner of yoga and Buddhist meditation, once told me an anecdote. He was in a meeting one day with one of his employees, a young woman who was a very efficient member of staff. She was nervous about a negotiation she was engaged in with one of their most important partners. My friend told her, "Just stop worrying, Laura. We're only here at work to enjoy ourselves."

If our attitude is geared towards creating beauty, the stress disappears because we stop working for money or to obtain material benefits.

Is there anything better in life than creating beauty? Once our basic needs are met – the only needs that really exist – why waste our time working? The only thing that's worth doing is to go straight for happiness and fulfillment by producing beautiful things. This will fill our lives like no other asset can.

Life is fascinating!

Many people are afflicted by the neurosis that life is uninteresting. I call this neurosis "dark glasses syndrome" because it's as if we were wearing sunglasses that make everything seem black and white when, in reality, things are wonderfully colored.

I can categorically state that life is always super fun and exciting. Why do I know this? It's simple: because this is how many thousands of people experience it, and they are not extraterrestrials! They are the same as everyone else; the only difference is that they know how to put on the right glasses, and they know how to activate their sense of fun.

And I have more proof. My own experience. At the age of forty-five, I now enjoy life more every day. People often say that the most exciting stage of life is youth, but I've come to realize that's not true. The best things in life come when you start thinking in the right way. Grandparents also have something to say about it. If we ask them, they advise us to make the most of every moment. For starters, they see us as too young! And at the end of their lives, they realize that every minute is exciting.

I've been lucky enough to be friends with the Catalan intellectual Josep Maria Ballarín, a modern priest, writer, and brilliant man. When he was ninety-four years old, one winter evening, over a bottle of cognac, we had the following conversation at his home in the Pyrenees:

"If I were born again, Rafael, I would live even more passionately! I would travel more, my religious devotion would be deeper, and I would make more art! My friend, I urge you to turn on that passion for me in your own life."

"Goodness, Josep Maria! But you've lived a great life! I don't think I'll ever reach your level," I replied with the vehemence that was characteristic of our well-oiled encounters.

"Don't say that, my friend! Focus on your tasks and perform them with all your passion. In no time, you'll be as old as me, looking back over your story. Life is a miracle that passes by in a flash."

His words will always stay with me, and they remind me of those of many other wise men and women, like Martín, a ninety-year-old from Barcelona who survived a Nazi extermination camp. In an interview with the Spanish nespaper *La Vanguardia,* he recounted how, after being liberated by the Americans, he spent a few exciting years in Vienna and Paris before returning to Spain. Martín explained how all the hardships he experienced in the war and the proximity of death made him aware of the miracle of life: the same miracle Ballarín spoke of. When he left the camp, he grasped life with both hands: he lost all his fears and set out to be the master of his existence. And since then, he has lived in that way: brilliantly.

Some time ago, I watched a film on television that taught me the same lesson: that life is a unique opportunity, and it is up to us to take it. The movie told the fictional story of a grandfather to whom something extraordinary happened: for a while, he regained his youth! Only his grandson knew that Grandpa was young again. The young man, thrilled at this new opportunity, started living a full life without fear, becoming the most popular young man in the area. The lesson for his grandson was clear: we humans easily forget that we are just passing through and that it's over in no time. If we remember this all day, every day, we give up false limitations and absurd complaints and start dancing on life's stage.

Yes, life's a party! And the music plays for everyone; you just have to know how to hear it.

In this chapter we learned that:

- "Tuning into harmony" means focusing on appreciating the little things and the beauty of our surroundings.
- This attunement brings well-being but also cultivates rational thinking. It involves not complaining and being happy with very little.
- "Reminder tools" can be bells, notes or anything that reminds us to put passion into everything.
- Asserting a manifesto for joy every day helps us find it.
- Trying to create beauty with all our actions increases our happiness.
- Putting ourselves in the shoes of an elderly person, we can see that life is always fascinating and there waiting for us.

7

New Rational Visualizations

"Excuse me," one fish said to an older fish, "can you tell me where what they call the 'Ocean' is?"

"Kid, the Ocean is where you are right now," said the older fish very seriously.

"What!? But this is all just water. You don't know anything – I won't stop until I find it!" the young fish replied as he swam frantically away.

Many years ago, I went to see a hypnosis show at a theatre in Barcelona. At the time, I was studying hypnotherapy with psychologists and doctors, and I wanted to see a showman who used these techniques in action. I'd been told that some people were very good at hypnosis, and I could learn from them.

I went with Joan, a friend of mine who was not involved in psychology. He works in banking, and in fact, he didn't even believe that hypnosis was possible. I explained that it had been proven to work for at least two hundred years and that I performed hypnosis myself in my early years as a psychologist. But none of my arguments convinced him.

The hypnotist, a certain Rugieri, was a man of forty or so, very thin, wearing a black suit. The guy had a mysterious air that he accentuated with atmospheric lighting and intriguing music. The first thing Rugieri did was some exercises to see who the most suggestible audience members were. He asked us to press our hands together and imagine we couldn't pull them apart. At the end of the experience, of the two hundred people who were in the theatre, about twenty couldn't unstick them. One of them was my friend. He was next to me with his hands together, laughing nervously.

"Rafa, I'm being serious. I can't pull them apart!" he said, annoyed.

I was splitting my sides with laughter because I hadn't expected it from him, of all people. There Joan was, a combative 15-stone executive as tall as a bear, shaking like a leaf at his own body's reaction.

The hypnotist asked those "affected" to go up on stage, and we gave them a loud round of applause. Joan looked at me from above, half amused, half scared. What followed was a typical stage hypnosis session: some ate lemons that tasted of pears, others believed they were on a nudist beach, and so on. But, to finish, Rugieri invited my friend to participate in one last experience: the highlight of the show. He made him believe that his body was as rigid as an iron bar.

"From now on, your legs feel completely hard," he said in a Transylvanian tone.

Joan's eyes were closed, and he was sweating slightly. His expression was strange as if he was dreaming. Rugieri went on. "And now your back is like a beam. You're made of iron!"

Then the hypnotist, very serious, asked three people from the audience to help him position a trestle on either side of my friend. And then... boom! Between the four of them, they lifted him and placed him on top: His neck on one trestle and his ankles on the other!

And there was a man who weighed 15 stone, supported by two pieces of wood, stiff as a board. I must admit, I was stunned, too. Joan was in this position for about five minutes while Rugieri offered some explanations to the audience. The truth is I was slightly on edge, not ruling out the possibility of an accident (and it was me who had persuaded him to go!). But nothing like that happened. In the end, the four of them lifted him up again as if he were a thick tree, standing him back on his feet.

After the show, we went for dinner, and Joan couldn't remember anything. I told him what happened, and he could hardly believe it! Other than that, he felt fine. He knew that he had been in a strange dream state for more than an hour and that, at first, he hadn't been able to separate his hands. But that was all.

UFOs, Marian apparitions, and Therapy

This story illustrates the power of imagination over the psyche because hypnosis is nothing more than a ploy to boost the imagination.

If we imagine acutely, our minds can reproduce events as if they were real to our senses: we can hear voices, feel intense heat or cold, and see objects and people that don't exist. It's not such a rare phenomenon! It can be achieved with certain drugs, through various fasting or breathing exercises, or by mere suggestion. Many people who have seen UFOs have, in fact, had one of these hallucinatory experiences, and the same thing can happen with religious apparitions. In Rugieri's show, a young woman thinks she is a Chinese actress in front of her fans and gives a short speech in made-up Mandarin. Her hallucination was so powerful that she spoke a fairly convincing version of Chinese. Of course, we applauded her like frenzied admirers!

Psychologists rarely use hypnosis because very few people are easily hypnotized – fewer than 10% – but the phenomenon teaches us that the imagination can be very useful when it comes to producing effects on our minds. In this chapter, we will see how we can use imaginative or visualization techniques to cultivate rational thinking. The goal is to vividly imagine the rational content that we want to insert in our minds until we achieve an almost hypnotic effect!

WAKING HYPNOSIS

In cognitive therapy, we perform *rational visualizations* to help us understand the logical principles we work with. This exercise is also known as *waking hypnosis* because we look for an effect similar to hypnosis but without the trance. The premises we work with are:

- We need very little to be happy
- Nothing is "terrible."
- Defects don't matter
- We can feel great no matter what happens

Visualization can also consist of imagining what we fear from another perspective. It's very useful to picture ourselves being happy in a feared situation.

Imagining equates to *experiencing* because when the brain imagines, it recreates events, and emotions arise. Serotonin and dopamine are released. Virtual memories are created.

On a mental level, it's almost like having genuine experiences! But there's one condition: visualization must have a rational basis and a logical argument so that we believe what we imagine. In other words, we can't deceive ourselves. We can convince or persuade ourselves but not delude ourselves.

Visualization is similar to what monks of all religions do when they pray or meditate. In fact, with their mantras, songs, incense, and candles, they create a pre-hypnotic state.

We will look at three different kinds of visualization that we can perform at any time and which encompass some of the basic principles of cognitive therapy. These three standard exercises will always be helpful, both as a preventive technique and to deal with a specific neurosis:

- The prisoner visualization

- The wheelchair visualisation
- The Saint Francis visualization

In all three, the aim is to imagine yourself being perfectly happy in precarious situations in order to combat complaining, necessititis, and terribblitis. Or, as we said in Chapter 2, to learn to tread lightly and appreciate our surroundings.

THE PRISONER VISUALISATION

This exercise consists of asking yourself, "If I had to do time in jail, what would I do to make myself happy?" We have to imagine various scenarios in which we are happy and satisfied with life... in prison!

I usually see myself building friendly relationships with other inmates, deepening my spirituality, and studying with passion (music, medicine...). The aim of this visualization is to understand that we can live fully with very little – even without freedom!

The logical conclusion from this visualisation is that my habitual complaints – my neuroses – make no sense. If I can be happy in prison, how can I not be happy without a partner, a steady job, etc? They are much smaller adversities!

Rational (or cognitive) therapy has many aspects in common with spirituality, unsurprisingly, because religions are also made up of concepts, ways of thinking, and values. Through the centuries, philosophy and religion have influenced each other.

Happiness Declassified

On the subject of religion, note how men and women of faith often wear certain clothes. A monk's habits or a Buddhist's robes, for example. Why do they do this? Not so they can be identified on the street, like police officers or firefighters. Their garments – or their shaved heads, for instance – serve another purpose. They are a message to themselves.

Habits serve the same function as a young rocker's tattoos. Their purpose is to remind the monk of his values and flag them. A nun's crucifix and coif help her adhere more strongly to the principles with which she wishes to live. If I were to go to prison, I would wear cheerful, modern clothes, but I might also wear a crucifix. With this, I would show myself and others my total commitment to solidarity and love. The modern clothes would send a message of joy and strength. And the crucifix, my readiness for deep friendship.

If I was in prison, I would use everything at my disposal to develop a strong value system. My mission would be to pursue a profound love of life and others.

Remember that the aim of visualizations is to become as committed as possible to the values of a *state of abundance,* as we called it in Chapter 2. This commitment is like the cornerstone of a house: we support ourselves on the pillar of our new cognitive values. In prison, this cornerstone would keep our minds in good shape. Think about it: if we could be happy in jail, how wonderful would life be right now, free of such extreme adversity?

THE WHEELCHAIR VISUALISATION

This exercise consists of imagining that we are unable to walk, visualizing life in a wheelchair: "If I had an accident and was left in a wheelchair, could I be happy?" The only answer is... yes! What would we do to achieve this?

I think I would go to live with other people in the same situation as me, perhaps near the beach, in a house without any architectural barriers. Together, we would find the necessary funds and design it with all the comforts we needed. We would live in a community, helping one another and also doing things for others. We would run personal growth programs for local residents, who would see our strength as an example to follow.

We would have an interesting, creative, mutually supportive life based on the principles of friendship, spirituality, a love of life, art, creativity... Could we be happy? Of course, we could! For well-equipped minds, there is virtually no serious impediment to achieving fulfillment.

THE SAINT FRANCIS VISUALISATION

I am not a Catholic, but I do admire one of their saints: Francis of Assisi. From an emotional perspective, I think this thirteenth-century monk deserves all our attention.

Francis was born in Assisi, a town in the present-day province of Perugia in Italy. His family was involved in the textile trade and enjoyed a privileged financial position. For the standards of the time, Francis was a rich boy: he led a carefree life, he studied but didn't work, and he was fond of music and love affairs until war sparked his conscience.

A conflict broke out between Assisi and Perugia, and, like the rest of his friends, Francis headed into battle. He was eager to demonstrate his gallantry. But what he experienced was very different from the chivalrous scenes he dreamed of death, cruelty, and madness in the name of an absurd patriotism, or worse still, hidden financial interests.

When he returned home, Francis was a changed man. He had seen death up close and was determined to live as meaningfully as possible in the service of love and happiness. Before long, he left the family home to retreat to the countryside. Not far from his town, there was a half-ruined church in an idyllic setting, surrounded by a green meadow dotted with leafy trees. Down the hill, a river flowed.

Francis's main occupation was to create beauty, returning it just as his senses received it from nature. He started rebuilding the beautiful church of rounded, polished, magnificent stones. During rests, he composed music that was joyful and odes to a youthful life full of luminous energy.

We could all emulate Saint Francis: give up the material life and live with very little. Or could we, at least, imagine it? We would live enraptured by nature's beauty, and our mission is to create more beauty. We would have no job, no responsibilities, and nothing to lose because we would have given up everything except Happiness with a capital 'H'; we would focus on friendship, music, and art. We would throw everything material, our image, and our pride in the bin once and for all.

Of course, we could! And in fact, mentally, we are going to do it. From now on, we will be committed to leading Saint Francis's inner life.

Francis was a champion of renunciation, and it is said that, at the end of his life, he declared: "Every day I need fewer things, and the few I need, I need them very little." If we are able to undertake this "blessed renunciation," we can become emotional superheroes.

The chronicles say that Francis's friends went to visit him at the hermitage where he had started living. They had been worried about his sanity. "Has he gone mad?" they'd wondered. When they got there, what they saw made a deep impression on them. Young Francis exuded energy and peace, something they immediately wanted to acquire themselves. Most of his friends joined him in his "madness."

We will also attract others with our loving energy because there's nothing more attractive than peace and happiness. Can we imagine ourselves in our new lives of renunciation, forging the best friendships – profound, precious, and authentic connections? Of course, we can!

In our visualization, we try to experience deep and beautiful connections with others because this, in turn, is something that nourishes us. In fact, it is a feeling that we can direct at everyone who inhabits the planet.

CRYING WITH INNER JOY

In the sphere of meditation – reflection, visualization, prayer, or whatever we want to call it – there are various depths. And the deepest state is something more than logical reasoning, an understanding, or a conviction: it's an inner experience.

The deepest cognitive – or spiritual – visualizations are so powerful that many people end up crying with emotion. Reaching this state, even people less inclined to show emotion break down in tears like children. And that's a good thing. It means we're experiencing sweetly overflowing emotions, and each of these moments leaves a mark on our psyche. They are the most powerful psychotropic drugs out there.

Some time ago, I watched a lecture on YouTube by Miguel Silvestre about travel and inner life. Miguel travels the world on a motorcycle and stars in the show *Diario de un nómada* ("Diary of a Nomad," www.miguelsilvestre.com) on the Spanish television channel TVE. I was touched by the moments in the lecture when Miguel Silvestre, a hardened traveler who has risked his life on countless occasions, started to cry while explaining his spiritual experiences. And he didn't care that he was standing in front of a hundred or two hundred strangers.

Because our inner life is where our most profound adventure takes place, why wouldn't we embark on it, navigate the most plentiful rivers and seas, and climb the most spectacular mountains? Let's visualize it, then, with as much energy as possible, and go out to conquer this beautiful world.

In this chapter we learned that:

- *Rational visualisations* help us understand the logical principles we're working with, which in turn helps us combat necessititis and terribblitis.
- The prisoner visualisation involves seeing yourself happy in the absence of freedom.
- The wheelchair visualisation is a way to perform the important act of letting go of the body and many comforts, without giving up fulfilment by doing so.
- The Saint Francis visualisation compels us to live a more authentic life, again one of renunciation, focusing on beauty and profound friendship.

Part Three:
Use it all!
8
Alchemists of Discomfort

Buddha was about to be killed by the famous bandit Angulimala. With the sword at his throat, he said:

"Grant me one last wish: cut off that branch."

Angulimala hacked at the branch, which crashed

to the ground. "And now? Are you ready to die?" the bandit asked.

"Just one more thing: put it back on the tree, please."

The bandit burst into laughter. "You're crazy if you think that's possible!"

"On the contrary, you are the crazy one because you think that destroying makes you powerful. Wake up and understand that the only great people are those capable of creating."

This chapter is one of the most important. It deals with a vital skill: the ability to *transform discomfort*. The strongest and happiest people are like alchemists, but instead of turning lead into gold, they transform uncomfortable situations into nice experiences to the point that they feel very comfortable again. Learning this cognitive skill will give our emotional strength a huge boost.

I have met a lot of people capable of this "alchemy of discomfort": great travellers, and religious or important (and ethical) leaders. Alchemists are like this:

- They have a lot of energy
- They're almost always cheerful
- They're calm people
- They're very positive and constructive
- They lead exciting and fulfilling lives
- They love themselves
- They're very creative
- They have a young spirit throughout their lives
- They relate to others brilliantly

And all these qualities are, to a large extent, afforded to them by their secret ability: their alchemy of discomfort.

But when our neuroses overwhelm us, the opposite happens: the discomfort is unbearable! We become hypersensitive, and everything bothers us, and that makes us bad-tempered, uncompromising, negative, sad, and weak. Our lives shrink because, running away from the discomfort, we end up limiting ourselves.

As ever, the good news is that change is possible with some persevering mental work: we will go from being overwhelmed by our neuroses to being adventurers who live life to the fullest.

WEARING EARPLUGS IN SEVILLE!

Sensitivity to discomfort is experienced with varying degrees of intensity, and we are all somewhere on the spectrum. Bad-tempered people are at the bad end; everything bothers them: noise, heat, cold, crowds, waiting... to unlikely extremes, in contrast to alchemists of discomfort, who know now how to be okay in any situation.

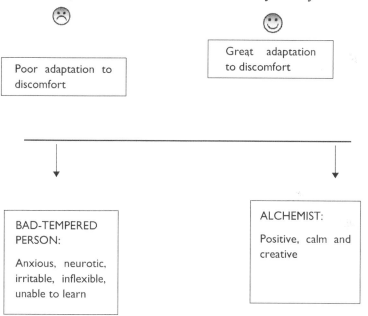

I have met people who experience discomfort as torture. On one occasion, I was doing a promotional event in Seville, and it was the turn of a fifty-something journalist named Lidia to interview me. We were in one of the city's loveliest bookshops, in the café area. After a few minutes, appearing upset, she stopped interviewing me and said to the press agent, "I'm sorry, I can't go on."

"Why not? Is there something wrong?" the agent asked, worried.

"It's so noisy in here! It's impossible to do the interview!" she exclaimed.

The agent – a woman in her thirties – and I looked at each other in some surprise because the place was quiet; we could talk easily. In fact, compared to Spain's usual mayhem, it was practically silent. In any case, we suggested going to another café where there was no one.

We continued the interview, but after a few minutes, I noticed that Lidia was wearing something in her ears, perhaps some hearing aids. I asked her, "Oh, are you wearing hearing aids? Maybe that's why the ambient noise bothers you. Maybe they're set too high."

"No! They're earplugs! I never go out without my plugs!"

Oh! Lidia was wearing earplugs in a city like Seville, which is nothing as noisy as Barcelona or Madrid. I inquired a little more, and the poor woman told me how she suffered from auditory hypersensitivity. She had a terrible time everywhere: in the newsroom, at home, in bars, on the bus... I smiled inwardly: I knew the problem well because I'd treated a lot of people with it.

We parked the interview and spent some time doing therapy. I explained that she had created her hypersensitivity herself by complaining about the noise. She had become bad-tempered because of her inner dialogue and her constant pursuit of comfort. An absurd and unnecessary comfort!

Lidia's is an example of neurosis caused by an attachment to comfort. And, as we said before, at the other end of the scale are the alchemists of discomfort, who are cheerful and well-disposed at all times. The perfect examples of these alchemists are the great adventurers who travel the world with a backpack and don't mind sleeping in a train station, walking all day under the sun, or spending days waiting in an airport. For them, every moment is an opportunity to learn, to do something creative – like writing a journal – or to have an interesting experience.

THE ALCHEMY OF DISCOMFORT SCALE

We can all determine how well we adapt to discomfort. We could position ourselves on a scale of 0 to 10, where 0 means being very sensitive to discomfort and 10 being almost impervious to it. And we can all improve our sensitivity: the more alchemy we achieve, the more flexible and the less neurotic we will become.

Improving this alchemy of discomfort is an emotional well-being exercise that improves all aspects of our inner lives. Our goal is to learn to be fine – increasingly so – in supposedly uncomfortable situations. And we can achieve this by changing the way we think about situations: instead of feeding the neurosis with our inner dialogue, we do the opposite.

Some typical discomforts that tend to make our lives a misery are:
- Long waits (at the doctor's surgery, in the supermarket queue, in a traffic jam)
- Noise (from a neighbour, in a restaurant)

- Heat or cold (how we complain in July and August!)
- Tiredness (for instance, having to stand on a bus at the end of the day)
- Tedium (in a dull lecture)
- Boredom (on a long journey at the airport)
- Contact with dirty or ugly places (a run-down neighbourhood...)
- Pain (a headache, stomach ache)
- Others' faults (colleagues, family)
- Crowds (on the underground, a packed beach)

Below, we will see how we can transform these situations into opportunities to enjoy ourselves, learn, and feel great. Our strength depends on it, so let's not miss a single opportunity to practise the alchemy of discomfort!

ARGUING IN FAVOUR OF COMFORT

When we grow impatient in a supermarket queue, it's because we tell ourselves things like: "Outrageous! What a badly run store!" or "I came to do a minute's shop, and it's going to take twenty. What a shambles!" In other words, we are the ones who light the fire of the feeling of discomfort. Our thoughts stir up discomfort like wicked little devils!

To put out the fire, we must draw on opposing arguments. For example, we tell ourselves, "Quietly waiting is a skill that sets civilised people apart from childish people," "I'm going to use this time for something gratifying like listening to music or replying to messages," or "I love waiting, it's time just for me that I can use to meditate."

Another strategy is to imagine similar scenarios in which we're unaffected by discomfort. For instance, if it's "horribly" hot, we can visualise ourselves living in Cuba or Indonesia, where the temperatures are extremely high. But our lives there are exotic: we're in a romance with a local, have an exciting job, and are leading a life of adventure despite the heat.

The strategy of visualising imaginary scenarios works because it makes light of our supposed discomfort on a logical level. If there's a situation in which hot weather is no impediment to having a great time – even if it's as a visitor to Cuba or Indonesia – then "the heat" itself is not so bad: it depends on the context and how we perceive a situation. And our minds get the message! With this exercise, we stop complaining and go into enjoyment mode. The quicker we change our inner dialogue, the better.

For every supposed discomfort, there is an alternative thought: pleasant scenarios, things to learn, and life adventures that show us that the situation is not so bad and that we can be happy regardless. Each time we manage to reverse a feeling of discomfort, we take another step toward emotional maturity.

DEAFNESS AS A TEACHER

Some time ago, something happened to me that illustrated the alchemy of discomfort. This anecdote is about my fantastic mother, who, while young at heart, active, and dynamic, has been losing her hearing in recent years. At one point, she decided to start using hearing aids. And, as I happened to know some manufacturers of these devices, I went with her to buy them.

But when she had them, she couldn't get used to using them. Hearing aids require some learning because you have to focus your mind to hear properly. This takes effort, and I suppose my mother got tired before she managed it.

She never wore them, and as her hearing worsened, it became more difficult to talk to her. There were a lot of conversations, such as:

"Mum, did you go to the cinema with your friends yesterday?"

"Son! How could you say that? There are no ants in my house!" she replied without realising that the question was about something else entirely.

Or a lot of what-what-what-what conversations:

"Hi, Mum. How's everything going?"

"What?"

"How is everything going?" I replied a little louder.

"What did you say?"

"Nothing. Don't worry," I would conclude.

The truth is, all these failed conversations became very tiresome, and for a few months, I tried to persuade her to use the hearing aids, mostly for her own good, because – in the long run – people tend to avoid those hard of hearing.

I would say to her, "Mum. You're going to isolate yourself because, even if you haven't realised it, people are already talking to you less. They get tired of it."

And she would answer, "My friends love me dearly! Unlike my children! I don't need to wear those gizmos!"

And after a while, in an ongoing flare-up of neurosis, the fact that my mother wouldn't make an effort to improve her hearing started to irritate me. I would say to myself, "Well, if you want to isolate yourself, that's your problem! I'm not going to repeat everything to her a thousand times! I'll visit less often, and that's that!" Without realising it, I'd become hypersensitive to the discomfort of talking to someone hard of hearing!

But luckily, something happened that taught me a valuable lesson. One Sunday, I went for lunch at her house and found my older brother Cesc there. I said hello, and we started chatting.

"How is everything, man?" I asked.

"GREAT!!! SPENDING A FEW DAYS HERE IN BARCELONA WITH MUM! I HAVE A WEEK OFF WORK!"

My brother was literally yelling at me.

"Hey!" I said. "*I'm* not deaf! Talk to me normally..."

"Gosh, sorry. It was because I've been talking like that all day for Mum," he apologised.

"What a pain her deafness is, don't you think?"

"No. Why? All you have to do is speak more loudly, look her in the face, and vocalise clearly. It's no big deal," he said matter-of-factly.

Whoa! His answer surprised me. He seemed completely relaxed, while I'd been annoyed by the issue for the last few months.

From that moment on, I tried to speak to my mother like he did... and it worked! All I had to do was adopt three simple measures: speak more loudly, vocalize clearly, and look her in the face so she could read my lips. In no time, I had adapted myself to speaking that way, and I haven't had any problems with my mother since. She understands me perfectly, and I learned something useful: to communicate better. In fact, television presenters follow the same rules to improve their diction.

However, the most important lesson I learned was that sensitivity to discomfort makes human beings become bitter and closes our minds to learning fascinating things. As soon as I stopped feeding my neurosis, protesting a trivial inconvenience, I adapted fully to the new situation and grew as a person.

BEING YOUNG TRAVELLERS

I have a friend, Josan, who is a great traveller. He has been to a lot of exotic places, mountaineering, exploring cities, and visiting ancient monasteries. Josan is fifty-five years old, but he appears much younger because he's in good shape: he cycles to work most days, travelling 40 miles there and back. He's fun, charismatic, and brilliant in his work as a journalist. And, not by chance, Josan has never attached much importance to comfort. He's a guy who enjoys nature, people, his work and life.

If we want to be like him, if we want to lead an exciting life, we need to ditch our absurd need for comfort. From time to time, it's great to get a massage, go to a spa, or take a nap. But only occasionally. For most of the day, it's better to be fit and open to discomfort as a way of adapting to life and enjoying it fully.

It will also allow us to enjoy relaxing and enjoy the pleasures of life much more because they're reserved for occasional, intense moments. "Good things come in small packages," the saying goes. It would be incredibly boring to always be comfortable all day long, in the same way that we would get tired of eating chocolate at all hours.

ENJOYING, RATHER THAN TOLERATING

There's a lot of talk in psychology about a concept similar to alchemy of discomfort: *frustration tolerance*. We say it's good to have a "high frustration tolerance." But I don't like this expression very much because it alludes to "enduring" or "suffering" and, with the exercise I propose, you don't suffer, but enjoy yourself. It's about opening your mind to the possibility of enjoying yourself in a situation that, on the face of it, is uncomfortable. For example, I feel great now that I have learned to speak to my mother more loudly, vocalizing clearly. I know I've learned a very useful skill and I like to practise it.

With *alchemy of discomfort*, we try to transform *discomfort* into *comfort*, not just *tolerate* it. Remember, it's all in the head! A different reading of the same situation can change it completely: lifting weights at the gym is a hobby; breaking rocks on the road is a punishment. Human beings have the option to transform any experience. Let's make use of this power. Down with "frustration tolerance" and up with "enjoying situations that are no longer uncomfortable"!

A MANIFESTO ON DISCOMFORT

I like manifestos. They are statements of intent that help us organise our thoughts and remain steadfast.

One of the most iconic manifestos in history was the one that Martin Luther King proclaimed in 1963, entitled *I Have a Dream*, in which he argued against racism and for equality. At the time, millions of people were deeply moved by his words, and it marked a wonderful step forward for human rights around the world.

My father has told me many times that, as a young man, he was able to watch the speech live on television. Although the racial problems of the United States were alien to him, the black minister who declared from Washington that love conquers all made a deep impression on him. The speech would shape his values in this respect for evermore.

In much the same way, we can also write or sign a manifesto in favour of alchemy of discomfort. It goes something like this:

A MANIFESTO ON (DIS)COMFORT

Today and for the rest of my life, I commit to a full, meaningful, and beautiful life full of passion.

From now on, I promise to take the miracle of life as it comes: cold or hot, sun or rain, snowstorms or tornadoes.

I want to lead the life of a traveller who explores, learns, and imbues themselves with joy.

If it is hot, I will welcome the weather and celebrate the arrival of summer. I will sweat cheerfully in pursuit of adventures that I will celebrate in spirited poems as if I were in Indonesia, like an intrepid Indiana Jones.

If I were in a poor and ugly place, I would imagine myself as an activist working to improve the neighbourhood: a passionate volunteer offering love and beauty to all the people living there. And I will love the place. There will be many fantastic people to connect with, and aesthetic concerns will be meaningless trifles!

If the noise is bad, I will realise that I can be happy there anyway. Human beings do not need silence to be happy! We have a mental switch to turn off noise if we ignore it. I can work, meet people, love others... participate in countless valuable activities! I will understand that noise is life, too.

Long waits and tired feet – stress or happiness, it's all up to me. I can be full of energy and love and do constructive things at all times.

Today and for the rest of my life, I will join the club of active, cheerful, and passionate people who are committed to a full and exciting life. I don't want much comfort – I don't need it! The best version of me is waiting for me in the best possible universe!

FASTING TO STRENGTHEN THE MIND

How amazing it is to get rid of any trace of attachment to comfort! To be like my friend Josan, the traveller, or like the legendary photographer Robert Capa, who covered events all over the world. Alchemy of discomfort is so good that many religious traditions practise planned renunciation.

Happiness Declassified

I have never fasted, whether for weight loss or as a religious practice. I've never been without food for a whole day. But it's not a crackpot idea. Sometimes, giving up sex, alcohol, going out, etc., can be beneficial because each time you fast, you hone your ability to enjoy other pleasures. It's like the phenomenon of the blind person who develops exceptional hearing: depriving ourselves of one pleasure opens up other pleasures.

Which is why, if we want to be free and increasingly fulfilled people, planned abstention can be very helpful.

Just for one day, instead of sex, have brotherly love; instead of the crude relaxation of alcohol, practise a musical instrument; instead of going to the cinema, begin some exciting studies...

Whoa! What amazing new pleasures a little smart fasting can bring!

In this chapter we learned that:

- Being hypersensitive to discomfort makes us bad-tempered and neurotic.

- We can all gain insensitivity to discomfort with the right kind of thinking: comfort does not bring happiness.

- Some strategies to desensitise yourself to discomfort are:

- Telling yourself that you can do valuable things in any situation.

- Visualising similar scenarios in which the discomfort doesn't matter.

- The key to living a full and intense life lies in *enjoying* and not merely *tolerating* situations.

9
Losing Performance Anxiety

In a remote village in the East, a woman found three elderly people sitting at the door of her house. They were wearing elegant clothes and conversing learnedly. Full of curiosity, she asked, "Can I help you?"

"We're travelling, and we wanted to stop along the way," they replied.

"Please, come in. I'll give you a glass of water," she suggested.

"We'd be delighted, though we can't all go in together. But invite one of us," the strangers said.

Just then, the woman's husband and young daughter came out to see what was happening, and the man said, "What is this nonsense? All of you, come in. Our village has always been hospitable."

In response to his insistence, one of them, with a long white beard, replied, "Dear friends, thank you very much for your kindness. But listen, my name is Wealth, and my companions are Success and Love. And the three of us cannot all go into a home together. Choose one, please."

The couple thought for a while until the husband said, "I would invite Wealth. His company will come in very handy."

"Success would be better – we've never known him!" the wife replied.

And the girl, who had been listening to everything, said, "Wouldn't it be better to invite Love in? Then the house would be filled with warmth!"

Her parents gave in to her plea and held out a hand to the old man named Love. But when he got up, his companions did the same and went to follow him. The woman asked, "But didn't you say you couldn't go in together?"

And Love replied, "Had Wealth gone in, the other two would have stayed outside. The same if Success had been invited. But since it was me who was chosen, my companions will visit your home. Because, dear friends, where there is love, there also tends to be success and wealth. Always follow your heart, and the other joys of this world will come to you."

Matías was a physiotherapist, and not just any physiotherapist – one of the best in Spain. He studied at important specialist centers abroad and treated elite sportspeople and famous dancers. Everything was perfect – in both his professional and his love life – but his problem was his damned *performance anxiety.*

Every new task, like writing a medical article or teaching a course, caused him stress. Faced with these challenges, as soon as they were proposed, almost automatically, he felt a stab in his stomach, and his mind was gripped by a fear of failure. It was very upsetting because his nerves afflicted him for several days or sometimes entire weeks.

And that wasn't all. He was also racked with anxiety each time he had to do his accounts for the tax authorities. In fact, he had decided that his wife would take care of his bank letters, receipts, and invoices because they caused the same symptoms: a stab in the stomach and a paralysing mental block.

During the first session, Matías told me he'd suffered from these nerves since university, and now, at thirty-five, he realized that they had severely limited his life. If it hadn't been for this problem, he would probably have stood out more in his profession, opening his own physiotherapy clinic, for instance. What was more, the accursed anxiety had gradually increased over the years.

In this chapter, we will see how to overcome this kind of performance anxiety, which is the most widespread emotional problem in Spain, with 80% of the population suffering from it in the form of work stress.

It also manifests in other areas like personal accounting – what I call "financial phobia" – and affects other activities like holidays (!); there are people who struggle with the idea of organising a vacation.

Performance anxiety centers on the responsibility of doing something that the person thinks they may fail. Many of us have experienced it at some time in our lives, but the good news is we can make it disappear forever. It will require us to completely change our philosophy about the "importance of things." Let's see.

NOTHING IS IMPORTANT

I was once on a television show with a large audience discussing work stress, and, by way of illustration, I said, "The problem with this anxiety lies in the fact that we attach a lot of importance to things that are unimportant. For example, work. What we don't realise is that the work we're doing right now is of no importance whatsoever."

"But Rafael, how can you say that? We all want to be good professionals!" the interviewer replied.

"Let's see," I said. "This television show, of what importance is it? None! If this programme disappeared, what would happen? Nothing!"

The journalist looked shocked. He didn't know whether I was serious or joking. I went on.

"No television program, not even television in general, is necessary for us to be happy. Fuck this show and television all over the world! Who cares?"

All that matters in life (once our basic needs – eating and drinking – are met) is to love life and others. This is a philosophical and spiritual truth – and a scientific one when it comes to the environment. And 99% of the jobs we do are of no importance because they have nothing to do with that. If they disappeared, as I said to that stunned journalist, nothing would happen. If there were no banks, schools, or even hospitals, we would probably live in natural environments, hunting and fishing. In this case, the planet would be able to survive, and we would regain our sanity at once. So why should we worry about work, which is a completely unnecessary thing?

THE RELAXED ACTRESS

A few years ago, I read the autobiography of María Luisa Merlo, the actress from Madrid. At fifty years of age, she underwent a kind of psychological and spiritual conversion: she went from being miserable and neurotic to being a calm and happy person. And she said that one of the collateral benefits of her new philosophy was that she had lost her fear of acting.

Theatre actors often suffer from stage fright. Before the curtain goes up, they feel nervous. Some get it so bad they throw up and are quite literally ill, but as the play progresses, they relax.

Well, after her "therapy," María Luisa realised it was no longer happening to her. To her surprise, before going out on stage, she felt perfectly relaxed and happy. And as she recounted in her book, she would say to young artists: "Don't tell me this is making you tense! Please, grow up! You don't think what we do here is important, do you? Don't make me laugh!"

With this, she wanted to say that the essential thing is to love life and fellow human beings. The other tasks we keep ourselves busy with are trivial. When we become fully aware of this, performance anxiety completely disappears. At work, we just play, have fun, enjoy ourselves, innovate, and have virtual orgasms of mental pleasure!

I am like María Luisa Merlo. When I go to give lectures in Spain and Latin America, I no longer experience the slightest negative emotion. Before giving a talk, I'm as relaxed as a child about to take his nap. In fact, I usually drink a coffee to wake myself up before going out to speak. And yet, as a young man, I was afraid of public speaking! But everything changed the day I became fully aware of what is really important in this life.

THE NON-TALK

For the last three or four years, I've been conducting personal experiments to illustrate the unimportance of things. In many of my talks, I go up on the platform, approach the microphone, and say, "Dear friends, I have something to confess to you. You'll have to forgive me! The thing is, I've been going out a lot at night this week. Every day! Drink after drink! It's been full-on. And this afternoon I suddenly remembered I had to give this talk. The truth is I haven't had time to prepare anything. So I have nothing to say to you."

I love seeing the expressions on people's faces after I say this. Some look at me, thinking I'm kidding. Others that I'm conducting some kind of psychological exercise. And the rest seem outraged. Despite the looks, I usually add, "So, friends, I think we'll have to do this together. I propose you ask or say something, and we start from there."

Happiness Declassified

In recent years, I have given ten to fifteen of these non-lectures, and I have to say they've been fantastic. There was a huge amount of participation, I felt great, and everyone was very satisfied. I would even say they have been the best talks I've given.

And why do I do this exercise? To prove to myself and others that my work is not important. That almost nothing is! That nothing would have happened if I hadn't given the lecture. That it has no bearing on what is essential in life; let's open our eyes once and for all!

My non-talk experience is inspired by something I witnessed in the early 2000s. The Buddhist lama Sogyal Rinpoche came to Barcelona to give a lecture before no fewer than a thousand attendees. My friend María, a close associate of the monk, provided me with a VIP pass.

Sogyal Rinpoche is an authority on Tibetan Buddhism, on par with the Dalai Lama. Hence, the room was packed. Those attending included some famous faces and more than one politician. I was in the second row, beside María, with a perfect view of the stage. Behind me, I could hear the hubbub of the audience.

The allotted time of 8 p.m. had arrived, and nothing was happening. And the minutes went by. Five minutes. Ten... some photographers got up to take panoramic shots of the audience and then sat down.

Fifteen minutes, twenty... almost everyone was looking expectantly at their watches because the monk didn't appear. Not even María or the other organisers knew what was going on.

Twenty-five minutes... no news from Rinpoche. People were beginning to think there had been some mistake. Maybe it wasn't the right day!

And finally, after a few more minutes, a procession led by the monk appeared at one end of the room. I remember his saffron-colored robe, his shuffling leather sandals, and the broad smile on his face. The man was calm, unhurried, happy. He even stopped to say hello to an acquaintance in the front row. He took us to the platform and gave a talk that lasted less than forty minutes. Of course, we finished at the scheduled time. It seems that to minimise the delay, Sogyal gave a shorter lecture.

When we left, we went for a drink, and I asked my friend, "Maria, is this normal for Sogyal Rinpoche? Does he usually keep the audience waiting?"

"Well, I'm going to tell you something: yes! And I think he does it on purpose because once or twice I've seen him outside the room, not doing anything, letting time pass."

I don't know for certain whether this good-natured monk wanted to convey with his attitude what I learned that day: that nothing is important except happiness. But in any case, I made that my lesson. Is there anything really critical in this life? Maybe a couple of things, and they have nothing to do with productivity, efficiency, or the madness of industrialisation.

BEING LIKE JOHN MCENROE

Some people will tell me I live in a privileged world, and we can't take things so lightly, but I have proof that we can. One piece of evidence is John McEnroe, the famous tennis player of the eighties.

McEnroe was number one for years. We all remember his outbursts of anger when the umpire took a point from him: "The ball's in!" he bellowed. But reading his biography, it's clear that McEnroe always enjoyed the sport with a lightness. Yes, he liked to compete, but he knew perfectly well that it was just a game and that the goal was to have a good time, to be happy.

When he left tennis, he opened a contemporary art gallery in New York and succeeded in his new venture as well. Once again, he decided to lead a life in which enjoyment came first. For McEnroe, life is a festival of pleasure, and our work can be our main source of entertainment. If we're successful, great; if things don't go well, we can have fun anyway. The main thing is the enjoyment, not the result.

From my own experience, I know that when we see responsibilities in this way, everything works out: we stop worrying and perform to our best. Let's imagine that we're all John McEnroes. That we're going to add a touch of fun and pleasure to our lives and all our responsibilities. That we're wearing our Nike trainers and sportswear to show the world that life is fun, and this is how we're going to live it: carefree, without fixating on whether we get it right. What matters is to be happy!

John McEnroe is one example to keep in mind, but in fact, most successful people have been able to activate enjoyment instead of obligation. And that is precisely their secret: without performance anxiety, it is much easier to shine. Those who challenge me on this give examples of sportspeople who behaved in the opposite way, like André Agassi, another US number one who suffered throughout his tennis career. He drew on suffering, pure willpower, and worry and managed to reach the top, but I'm certain he would have accomplished much more if it were not for the neurotic madness that afflicted him. Obligation and worry are mediocre forces, and, worst of all, they lead us down the path of unhappiness!

MATURITY MEDALS

An executive from a large multinational once came to me for therapy. Mónica was about forty years old, and she had just been promoted to a coveted position on the company's board of directors. Her salary was astronomical, and she travelled all over the world. The problem was that, since she had taken on her new responsibilities, reporting to a senior American boss, she had been feeling stressed for the first time in her life.

The new boss was very demanding, and Mónica felt pressured. In one of the sessions, she told me, "In Paris two days ago, I presented the investment strategy for the next year. It went okay, but I've been super tense all week. I've struggled to sleep."

"Let's see. What if the presentation had been awful, the worst-case scenario?" I asked vehemently.

Mónica laughed at the thought of doing it extravagantly badly.

"Well, I guess they would have caught my attention and asked me to do it again another day," she replied.

"Okay. Imagine that from now on, all your presentations go wrong! Imagine they're all an unavoidable failure," I suggested.

"Then they'd fire me for sure, Rafael!" she said, laughing again.

"Well, then. Would that be the end of the world? What would you do with your life?" I asked very seriously since we were talking about our most sacred values.

Mónica thought about it for a moment and turned her serene gaze to me.

"It wouldn't be so bad. They would compensate me very generously, and I could find a new job."

The following week, she explained to me that for the first time in many months, she'd managed to release the pressure and completely relax, all thanks to this exercise. But our work was far from done. We continued to talk about her performance anxiety.

"I believe that a person's worth is not in doing a certain job well but in our capacity for love," I explained. "When we're about to die, only our acts of love will have left a mark on us..."

"That's true, Rafael," she said, serious and thoughtful.

"So, if we strengthen this value system, failing at mundane things has no effect on our self-esteem. Do you see? Failure and success are not what's important in life: all that matters is loving and enjoying ourselves while we're alive!"

Mónica nodded because as she internalised these ideas, she felt more relaxed and at peace. I went on.

"I think we could all go to work, fail, and be proud of our mistakes. With our heads held high! It would demonstrate that, in our value system, all that counts is our ability to love."

Mónica, who was a believer, connected these ideas to her religion, and her facial expression grew ever more relaxed. She was finding deep peace. I continued.

"And every mistake we make could be a medal on our chests. Proudly, every error would amount to an award in the most important career in life: that of being a person."

"Oh, Rafael! This really hits home with me. You're absolutely right! I don't know how I lost sight of it."

I've worked with a lot of executives who are stressed at work and, after changing their value system, transformed dramatically. There was one in particular who became a role model for others within his company, even his boss!

The first time I saw him, he was a bundle of nerves. He slept terribly. At weekends, he was obsessed with work. All he could think about was retirement! But after a few months of rational work, he was a different person. His boss – the general manager in Spain – started inviting him to lunch every Friday to receive rational teachings. His peers would also go to him when they were stressed.

But if we want to experience such a profound change, we must undergo a radical mental process. To the point that we turn what used to be shameful mistakes into medals of happiness!

RADICAL HUMILITY: THE KEY TO WELL-BEING

There's a quality that seems to have gone out of fashion, and it's important for mental health: humility. I think it's a basic virtue, but for it to bring us calm at all times, it must be a deep and authentic humility. Half measures won't be enough here! I'm referring to the humility of a person who doesn't want to be more than anyone else but just another person. When we're neurotic, we often get the idea that we have to stand out to "be someone." Otherwise, we're "failures". But nothing could be further from the truth. To be happy, the essential thing is our ability to have a good time to appreciate the little things.

When it comes to relationships, this translates into having sincere and loving friends, which has nothing to do with achievements. We all want to have friends who treat us like equals, who we can hold by the shoulder like when we were kids. People who are easy to love.

When we regain our mental health, we no longer want to stand out or be more than anyone else. We can have successes, but they will end up as mere anecdotes. The spotlights and applause will have lost their significance.

Money and renown are nothing more than collateral outcomes of living with love and enjoyment. But, if we want to be strong and happy, our relationships must be based on the deepest humility, knowing how ridiculous it is to have a need to shine. All that counts is playing, loving, enjoying!

Some time ago, I had a patient who was a lecturer in anthropology. Miguel had one of those generous old university contracts that many would envy: he earned more than three thousand euros a month for six hours a week of teaching. Besides that, he could carry out research in his field or not. No one forced him.

But despite everything, Miguel was miserable. He slept terribly. He spent many nights awake working. And his mind was always full of negative ideas about his colleagues and boss. Miguel believed that his superior, a leading scholar in the field of anthropology, thought he was a nobody and made it clear in meetings.

As if that were not enough, he was very insecure about his teaching ability. Facing students made him nervous, and if they showed signs of being bored, he told himself he was a "failure." In other words, his job was more like hell than the paradise it could have been for many.

And, in line with what we've described here, his therapy involved realizing that "knowing a lot," "being clever," "performing at work," etc. are silly needs unbecoming of a mature person. They can get in the bin!

I suggested a behavioural exercise:

"Why don't you make yourself a T-shirt with a slogan that says, "I'm the worst anthropologist in the world" and wear it to all your classes?" Miguel laughed at the crazy suggestion. But I insisted. "Because if you really felt that it doesn't matter, you'd become the best lecturer in the university: a philosophically mature person who tries to teach the little he knows with humility. With warmth. Without putting on airs. Putting love above everything else. I'm certain the students would adore you!"

THE CRAZIEST PROFESSIONS, RANKED

My experience as a psychologist has allowed me to meet a lot of people from very different professions. I ended up getting to know them quite well because they told me about their private lives and, often, their work relationships. Over the years, a curious map of what we could call "the craziest professions" has formed in my mind. The occupations in which there tends to be the most neurosis.

And this is what I've found. The wackiest tend to be:

1. Judges and other court employees
2. University lecturers
3. Classical musicians (concert performers and opera singers)
4. Actors
5. Doctors

What these professions have in common is that their members tend to put too much pressure on themselves to "think too much of themselves."

This happens among what I call "the capped nutcases": judges, lecturers, and doctors.

Not by accident, intrigues are the order of the day, to the point that the atmosphere can become strained when, in reality, they're beautiful professions. They don't embrace the wonder of their work. And there's nothing worse for mental health than so-called "personal prestige"! It's one of human beings' most unhinging made-up needs.

I will never stop being surprised by the internal quarrels that take place in the courts: judges and court clerks at each other's throats, generally because of absurd demonstrations of power. The poor users of the courts often pay the price for these cockfights.

Departmental meetings in Spanish universities are frequently bedlam (I know them well because I've worked in a couple of universities). A good friend of mine, an economics lecturer, describes them: "They fight like hyenas over a ridiculous purse of funds and hate each other because they believe there can only be one genius." Poor wretches: they don't understand that we're all geniuses and that genius is found in our ability to love.

And another cursed field: classical music and opera, which lays waste to the mental health of thousands of music students around the world. Absurdly, technical perfection is pursued when perfection isn't beautiful – it's unnatural! It's also an impossible invention of a tortured mind that doesn't work. I've met many of these professionals, applauded on stages all over the world, who secretly hate what they do.

And finally, my medical colleagues, with whom I work closely, insist on calling one another "doctor such-and-such," putting on airs that are actually pathological. I have never understood this strange custom, which belongs in *Alice in Wonderland*. All they're missing are the top hats, like the white rabbit. Why don't they call each other by their names and surnames like everyone else?

But all these airs of grandeur are only to our detriment. We have to be aware of this if we want to be truly strong and happy. No one, however complex or laudable their work, is anything more than a human being, naked in the world, no different from an Amazonian tribesperson. No one is more than anyone else! At least, not if they want to remain sane.

In this chapter we learned that:

- Work is just an occupation to entertain us. No job is truly important.
- If we approach work with a lightness, enjoying it, the results will be excellent.
- We can wear our mistakes as medals that tell us what our values are in life.
- Radical humility is the basis of love between people. No one who believes themselves superior can be fully happy.
- We can only achieve peace of mind and enjoyment at work if we embrace this philosophy in a very profound way. There's no middle ground in this.

10
Losing Our Fear of Illness and Death

King Solomon was rich and powerful, but he was never satisfied. "I often find myself anxious," he would tell his counsellors. "If things go well, I fear they will go awry. If I have a problem, I fear it will never be fixed. I have dreamed that there is a ring that grants knowledge and peace of mind. Find it for me. You have until the end of the year: six months."

The counsellors set out: they asked the best jewellers of Damascus, Babylon, and Egypt; they consulted the most travelled merchants, diplomats, and even necromancers... But no one had heard of such an object.

Time passed, and Solomon constantly asked, "Have you found the ring yet?"

"Not yet, my lord," they always replied. Finally, the six months came to an end. Everyone had given up except the youngest counsellor. The night before the end of the year, he was roaming the streets. He couldn't sleep at the thought of appearing empty-handed before his king.

In the morning, he found himself wandering through the city's poorest neighbourhood and, outside a house, he saw an old man setting up a jewellery stall. In one last attempt, he asked him about the ring.

The old man thought for a few minutes and, smiling, he took a simple gold ring from a bag and engraved some words on it. The young counsellor took it, read the inscription, and exclaimed, "Yes, this is Solomon's ring!"

A few hours later, in the great hall of state, Solomon asked his ministers, "Have you found my ring?"

"We have it, my lord!" said the young man triumphantly.

Solomon put it on and read the words inscribed on it: "This too shall pass."

Health is an issue that affects us all. Sooner or later, neurotic or not, it will give us a shock. And when it happens, it's better to be well prepared. Death lies in wait, and sickness is always with us.

In the fifteenth century, in his *Coplas por la muerte de su padre* (Verses on the Death of his Father), Jorge Manrique said:

Remember the sleeping soul, arouse the mind and awake contemplating how life goes by, how death comes so quietly [...]

In this chapter, we will learn to face sickness and death like champions of emotional intelligence, whether it's us, family, or friends who are affected by a serious illness. And we'll see that there is a truly constructive and calm way to approach the subject, one that enables us to take the best care of ourselves so that, when the day comes, we can be no more and no less than the best sick people in the world. Or, in the end, die happy.

In my work as a psychologist, I have been surprised more than once by the incredible ability that some people have to put aside any worries, even the most dramatic ones like illness and death! But of course, I've seen cases of the opposite: when the slightest possibility of being ill ravages someone's mind until they're exhausted with worry.

So what's the mystery? How is the former achieved?

DEATH IS NOTHING TO FEAR.

The first premise when it comes to losing our fear of illness and death is to be persuaded by the fact that, sooner or later, we all have to die and that, therefore, it's absurd to be afraid of it. Human beings, in nature, are serene when they contemplate their own end!

This statement might seem surprising because we have been made to think that death is something ugly, negative, wrong, and tragic. You just have to visit a cemetery to see this. They're dismal places! In fact, the very existence of cemeteries is the result of an irrational belief that death is bad. Undoubtedly, in a rational world, they wouldn't exist because they're absurd places where some bones are buried to be periodically visited. Let's get rid of cemeteries once and for all!

The logical thing would be to dispose of bodies without them leaving a trace since the dead person has gone, never to return. And if we think about it, the most beautiful thing is their natural decomposition: rich food for bugs of all kinds. But we have built cemeteries to visit the dead as if they lived in those stupid tombs. When people die, they are gone! What are we doing visiting those stones? This surreal behaviour is a product of a neurotic rejection of death. Because death is beautiful, it's an indispensable function of this wonderful life, and there is nothing to regret about it. In fact, it should be celebrated as part of nature's magical flux.

Today, as it happens, I'm writing these lines from the cafeteria of the National Archaeological Museum in Madrid after visiting the exhibition on Egypt with its sarcophagi and mummies. And I can't help but think of the absurd attachment Nefertiti and her contemporaries had to live. There's nothing better than dying! I find it ridiculous that they built pyramids to deceive themselves. Who wants to go on stuck in a box wrapped in bandages? Dying is great!

The main argument for not fearing illness or death is precisely this: to stop swimming with the tide of the society inherited from the Egyptians and earlier cultures to embrace a more ecological concept, like that of native Americans, for whom death is a desirable and completely normal event like birth, making love or bathing in a crystalline lake.

In reality, living beings die, and we don't know what fate awaits us. And that's fantastic simply because it's what's natural. Everything natural is good!

Faced with our parents' old age, the death of a loved one, or any illness, let's keep in mind that nature is wise and beautiful, and changes, in all their natural facets, are fantastic – albeit mysterious – and inevitable. And after making my debut a few chapters ago in the art of manifesto writing, here's another:

A MANIFESTO FOR DEATH

When my parents die, I will have a party with drinks as strong and as intense as life itself.

I will give their clothes and photos to the poor and only keep whatever memories of them fit in mind.

And I will set out to live my life with the intensity it deserves because, before long, we will all cross the river.

When I see death coming, I will ask those around me to drink in my honour.

I'm already calling at heaven's gates; I know this, and it makes me appreciate this sweet, starry night even more.

THE PRESENT MOMENT

A Buddhist monk returned to his old monastery after meditating for ten years in the solitude of the mountains. As soon as he arrived, he ran to see his old master. He knocked on the door.

"Master, it's Tenzo. I'm back. Can you see me?"

"Of course, my child. Come in," the old man replied.

The monk took off his sandals and entered his beloved mentor's cell. He sat on the floor and said, "Master, I have been meditating for ten years, and I have reached enlightenment. I can answer any spiritual question now."

"Let's see," the old man said warmly. "Tell me, on what side of the door did you leave your sandals?"

Tenzo tried to remember where he had left his footwear but could not find it.

At that moment, the smiling master said, "Can't you remember where you put your own sandals just a minute ago? Dear Tenzo, you're still not living in the present moment. Come back in another ten years."

The second argument to stop fearing illness and death is the importance of the present.

If we understand that the present is the only thing that requires our attention, death will no longer be a problem because it always happens in the future.

Happiness Declassified

When I was young, I would go out at night every weekend without exception. I loved meeting my friends, talking about our week, debating, flirting, drinking, dancing, and partying until dawn. These nights out were like small ceremonies in celebration of friendship, life, fun, and youth.

More than once, inspired by the sweet tiredness of the day, with dawn about the break, I walked home through Barcelona's Parc de la Ciutadella. In that moment of total calm, I appreciated the loving immensity of life, and I couldn't have cared less how long I would live for: a day, a year, a century? All that mattered was the present moment.

It's clear that happiness and spiritual strength lie in the present. Today is a miracle that requires our full attention. Human beings who live with intensity are only interested in the now. In our moments of ecstasy (on a mountain, making love, etc.), none of us care what will happen tomorrow. And this is the way of living that calls to us.

In other words, our fear of illness and death vanishes when we're focused on today, committed to living in ecstasy in the present.

There's a clear link between happiness and an indifference to death. It goes something like this:

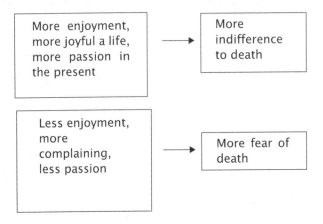

TRANSCENDENCE AND ETERNITY

The Roman poet Horace wrote, *"Carpe diem, quam minimum credula postero,"* which could be translated as: "Seize the day, trust not tomorrow." Horace was a very spiritual man, and his appeal to live in the present was a product of his moments of religious harmony. When we tune into spirituality, we are overcome by a kind of sense of eternity that leaves death without content or meaning.

When I was young, I travelled with some of my best friends around the Balearic Islands. It was May. We explored coves, mountains, and villages. We met interesting people, played music under the starlight, and, more than once, slept on the beach after an improvised hippy party. In the day, we were bathed in radiant sunlight, and at night, the sound of the sea lulled us to sleep. In Formentera, we went to visit an elderly farmer. The woman was a family friend of my friend Lluc, who was from there. The old lady introduced us to all of her sheep by name and invited us to dinner. She was an endearing person. To thank her, Lluc and Felip played a couple of traditional island songs on the instruments they had with them. They were professional musicians. And the woman, to my surprise, joined in, signing in Balearic Catalan. It was beautiful. Felip's guitar, Lluc's violin, and the folk singer were in perfect harmony with that idyllic setting.

That night, when we were returning to our hostel at three or four in the morning, I looked up at the starriest sky I'd ever seen. There was total calm; the air smelled of the island's magical vegetation.

In a state close to nirvana, Lluc said with feeling, "We're immortal. Can you feel it, guys?"

Neither Felip nor I added anything. We didn't even look at each other. We walked on with the conviction that the experiences of that trip would in some way extend through time on a kind of second plane where good things exist in parallel. And many minutes later, Felip blurted out, "Of course we're immortal!" And he meant it.

CONSCIOUS AND ETERNAL ACTS

Yes. We can all turn our backs on death. It's very easy! Just don't give it your attention. Our fear stems from the fact that everyone says it's horrible. It's a shared neurosis, a collective nonsense.

I have a friend named Elisa who was once diagnosed with a tumour that appeared malignant. In the end, it wasn't, but while she waited for the test results, she remained as happy as ever. I asked her how she managed not to worry. I imagined that her strong Christian faith was helping her, but she replied, "Rafael, I just focus on the present. Today is a miracle overflowing with wonders. If I tried to figure out whether I'll live or die tomorrow, I would miss today."

And she was sincere! These weren't new-age self-help affirmations.

Life is made up of "eternal" and "mechanical" acts. And I firmly believe that a single beautiful act – a meaningful, loving one – is more important than a thousand labours without beauty, without a legacy. Our spiritual minds tell us that the beautiful leaves an undying trace, an eternal imprint. The mechanical, on the other hand, is lost. If I knew I was going to die tomorrow, like Elisa, I would choose to focus on producing an "eternal act": writing a delightful poem, appreciating the colours of the afternoon, going for a walk with a friend, or in other words, living with passion. Fuck tomorrow! It's not my concern. My attention is fixed on beauty, on eternity.

146

ILLNESS DOESN'T EXIST

In my book *Las gafas de la felicidad* (*The Happiness Glasses*), I write at length about illness and how to understand it so that it doesn't take away a single shred of happiness. The strategies I outline to achieve this are:

a) Seeing illness as another of life's adventures

b) Wanting to be the best sick person in the world

c) Enjoying mutual support by joining patient organisations

But now I would like to add one more key.

One of the reasons why the appearance of an illness makes us miserable is because we tell ourselves, "It's bad luck." We usually look around us, compare ourselves to people who appear healthy, and feel bad about ourselves.

But this exercise is irrational because, once through our first flush of youth, we're all already sick. Or, to put it another way, no one is. Illness is simply a feature of life. If, every time it appears on our horizon, we tell ourselves, "This is normal; it happens to everyone," we can process it in a much better way. After the age of twenty-five or so, people begin to lose their health, develop short-sightedness, and their backs hurt... and that's okay! We can continue to enjoy life as always, as happy elderly people show.

Good travellers see any situation as a learning opportunity. If their money and documents are stolen, they don't stop to cry. They see it as another step on their journey and set out to resolve it as creatively as possible. Then, it will be part of their journal of adventures, their trove of glorious stories.

Exploring the Himalayas, for example, has its mishaps, moments of exhaustion, incidents, and scares, but it's also full of learning experiences and moments of ecstasy. Illness is really just one of these life events that we can turn into beautiful feats. Nothing to complain about.

FEARLESSNESS

At the same time, befriending death reduces our fears in general. Any fear – because they are always the result of attachments. If we're afraid of public speaking, it's because we *desperately need* to succeed in the task. Because if we don't care if a talk goes badly, there's nothing to fear.

And the same goes if we get nervous about buying a house. What are we really afraid of? Losing money if things go wrong? No big deal! We've never needed more than a sandwich and a bottle of water.

And, of course, losing our attachment to life itself makes any fear evaporate. The marvellous fact that we'll be dead tomorrow is the best de-stressor. Once in the grave, everything will be more than lost. So, what sense do everyday worries have?

WHAT HAPPENED TO SOPA DE CABRA?

A good exercise to help us lose our attachment to life is to notice how quickly time passes for the musical heroes of our youth. Recently, I happened to see a promotional photo of the band Sopa de Cabra ("Goat Soup"). They were very successful in Catalonia in the early nineties, when I was twenty years old. They were a rock group with a very slick, rebellious image: long hair, leather clothing, and defiant looks.

The promotional photo I saw in the newspaper was for the group's comeback album. They had been retired for twenty years. But the interesting thing – for the purposes of this chapter – was that the musicians shown in the portrait were different guys. These sixty-somethings didn't look anything like the heroes of my youth! They were gentlemen who looked like they had been taking care of their grandchildren all morning. What had happened to the real Sopa de Cabra?

Life is over in two shakes. A few years on the crest of the wave, selling thousands of records, producing music with huge creativity, and boom! It's over. Next, please! It's curious that we only notice the transience of existence at certain times, like when we see old and new photos of someone.

We're unaware of the proximity of death because we tend to think that our existence will be extremely long. We act as if we were going to live for a thousand years. We deceive ourselves, and the bad thing is that we miss the wonderful feeling of liberation that a sense of imminent death brings.

To benefit from the proximity of death, there's nothing better than befriending it, bringing it to mind more often, and imagining that we could allow ourselves to die peacefully, lost in the mountains, tomorrow!

GETTING LOST IN NATURE

I have a good friend, Gorka, a mountaineer by profession, who has faced the man with the scythe many times. The stumps where several of his fingers should be are souvenirs from these encounters. Once, in a mountain refuge, over a bottle of sloe liqueur, he explained, "The last time I was on Annapurna, I got lost near Camp IV and had to spend the night in an ice rift. At first, while I was preparing a plastic sheet that would serve as a tent, I was shitting myself. I've never felt despair like that in my life. I knew that if the temperature dropped, I would freeze to death right there. But then I had a thought that helped me relax. I told myself, 'Gorka, I think your time has come. It's fine. Mother Nature will take you.' I got in my sleeping bag. 'You've had some amazing experiences; remember the lakes under the peaks, the blue skies, the starry nights. You're going to join all of that.' I cried with emotion, and I think the tears froze as they fell. But I swear to you that, all of a sudden, I went into a serene and lucid state that I've never experienced again in my life. I drifted off and had an incredibly restful sleep. The next day, I found my way back. I was actually very close, but I never would have been able to find it at night."

As Gorka noted, Nature is the vast and unfathomable mother of each and every one of us. It brings us into the world and reclaims us, and that's how it has to be.

Faced with any fear – a presentation at work, getting lost in a dangerous neighbourhood of Bogotá, waiting for the results of some decisive medical tests... – we can serenely accept the certainty that, before long, we will be dead. In this moment, we can be mountaineers like Gorka and let ourselves die lost in the mountains.

Let's imagine we're astronauts contemplating the world's sphere from a spacecraft. Everything rotates at a harmonic pace, and all is well. Our death is okay, too.

For Gorka, his death will be another journey, a new adventure through the wilds of nature. As he told me that day in the refuge, on all his journeys, he goes deep inside himself because there, in the steep mountain passes, lies his soul, everyone's soul. What is my indomitable Basque friend if not a part of the universe? That's how he feels. And so do I, especially when I breathe the icy mountain air or let the water of a transparent sea caress my body. Death is my sister, as is the rain, the thick oak trees, and the whale I once saw rising, colossal, from the water.

Fear can invade our minds like an angry wave and make them reel. But we can tame it. You bet we can! Sit with the worst of the storm –

no running away. The mind searches for ways out like a person possessed, but the first thing to do is calm down.

When fear bares its teeth, I will stop and think of my own death. Of how I will welcome it, lost in the mountains.

THE DEATH OF LOVED ONES

In my previous books, I provide some cognitive methods for coming to terms with the death of a loved one, but I want to add one more here. When a family member dies, we often grieve the loss of a great source of love. This is most obvious with the death of a parent (and even more so when it's our mother). Because it's true that no one will love us like a mother: no one will be so willing to give everything for us. And when she goes, we feel that we're losing something precious without remedy.

The antidote to this sadness is to consider that other human beings can also be incredible sources of love. To surprising extremes! Losing an important person in our lives can free us to open ourselves up to others. And we can do so with as much intensity as we want.

In reality, we could all love one another like mothers love their children. Wouldn't a world like that be great? I'm convinced that we could do it. It doesn't mean giving everything to everyone – even a good mother shouldn't do everything for her child – but it does mean wholeheartedly desiring their happiness, holding our hearts out to them, and making a commitment to others. Not only does love for others activate a great channel of inner enjoyment, but it also makes others imitate us and give us back large doses of love.

We human beings are designed to open ourselves to showers of love – we can't help it! When we receive them, we tend to send out our own. And before we know it, we're bonded together in loops of love.

Let's open up to this kind of motherly love! Our emotional brains will respond by flooding themselves with serotonin and dopamine. Yes, the happiness substances.

In this chapter we learned that:

- The main mistake we make when facing death and illness is to see them as something bad. An ecological outlook helps us view them with respect and admiration.
- Focusing on the present keeps our fear of death and illness at bay.
- Illness is another of life's adventures and being "the best sick person in the world" is a fantastic challenge.
- Being aware that we will all die soon activates a sense of *carpe diem.*
- A good strategy when facing any fear is to visualise ourselves dying serenely in the mountains.
- When a loved one dies, we can open ourselves up to deeply loving others.

11
Overcoming Our Fear of Ridicule

When he was young, Nasreddin crossed the border every day with his donkey's baskets laden with straw. He was a smuggler, and when he arrived at customs, the first thing he did was confess, "My name is Nasreddin, and I am a smuggler."

The guards searched him again and again. They checked his clothes and load: they stuck their bayonets into the straw, submerged it in water, and even burned it to see if there was anything hidden in it. But they never found anything.

Meanwhile, Nasruddin's wealth continued to grow. When he finally became a mullah, he was sent to a far-off village, and he gave up smuggling forever.

One day, in that remote place, he met one of the customs officers from his youth, who couldn't resist the temptation to ask, "You can tell me now, Nasreddin, what were you smuggling that we could never find?"

"Donkeys," the wise man replied.

This ancient story of Islamic origin exemplifies how what is important to some is often irrelevant to others. If we have strong values, our minds will be occupied with what's important, regardless of what others think. To overcome our fear of ridicule, we just have to be clear about what is essential: this focus will make us emotionally strong.

155

A PERVASIVE FEAR

Shame is a toxic emotion that plagues many people. The people most affected are those who suffer from social anxiety, are reluctant to mix with others for fear of being hurt or making a fool of themselves, living in near isolation.

But to a lesser extent, it also affects many young people who steer clear of the opposite sex for fear of rejection.

Just think of how many people lament not getting lucky in their first twenty or thirty years of life!

Another typical case where this fear is manifested is public speaking. Eighty percent of people say that the idea of giving a speech terrifies them!

To some extent, the fear of ridicule limits almost everyone. So many of us never undertake a project for fear of failure and what they will say! It's like what John Lennon said: "Life is what happens while you are busy making other plans." In short, shame is one of the big limiters in our lives, and freeing ourselves from it gives us enormous advantages. And using the right cognition, we can become completely shameless.

THE DAY IT SLIPPED OUT

Something happened to me once that could be described as embarrassing. In reality, it wasn't because shame is an absurd emotion, and nothing is embarrassing, really, except to our minds. As we will see in this chapter, as we become more rational, we simply stop experiencing this feeling.

As a young man, I got together with a very sweet and beautiful girl. I'd been pursuing her for months, and finally, she agreed to have dinner with me. We had a great time. As I headed home that night, I thought, "Wow, how lucky am I? I think she likes me!" I was so excited I could barely sleep.

Our second date was also wonderful. We went to an Indian restaurant for dinner. And afterward, Elena said, "We can have our last drink at my place, which is nearby."

"Sure, why not?" I replied, hiding my excitement. Elena took me to her apartment, and we slept together. It was beautiful.

But in the middle of the night, around 3 a.m., a nightmare woke me up. I turned my head and saw Elena's lovely silhouette there. Comforted, I went to give her a furtive kiss. But as I stretched out my neck to reach her, I noticed a strong smell. What the heck was it? It stank! In milliseconds, in an ultrasonic mental exercise, my brain gave me the answer.

I'm sure my face must have twisted out of shape. I quickly lifted the sheets, and there it was, beside me, a disgusting puddle of feces. I'd shat myself!

I covered myself again at full speed, this time up to my ears, so the stench wouldn't escape. And it all became clear: the spicy Indian dinner had disagreed with me, and, fast asleep, my bowels had loosened. Oh God, this couldn't be happening to me! How gross! What an idiot! What would Elena think of me?

I didn't know what to do. I couldn't clean it up without her knowing. So I decided to wake her up.

"Elena! Please, wake up," I said, tapping her on the shoulder.

"Hmm? What time is it?" she asked with her eyes closed.

"It's late. Hey, can you go out of the room for a moment? Just a moment..." I said as I pushed her out of bed.

My intention was to get her out as quickly as possible so she wouldn't see the disaster. Then I'd clean it all up.

"What is it?" she said, opening her eyes wide. Then she held her fingers to her nose. "Jesus, what a stink!"

The game was up! After that, the terrible events unfolded as follows: I got Elena out of the room and, through the door, asked her to go and sleep on the sofa. I told her I'd had an accident and I wanted to clean it all up BY MYSELF. She insisted on helping me, but it goes without saying I didn't let her.

I didn't sleep for the rest of the night. I washed the sheets and, what was harder, the mattress. My foul-smelling bowel movement had penetrated that far. I scrubbed it with water and soap and every cleaning product I could find in the apartment. Then, I dried it thoroughly with a hairdryer and repeated the operation several times until there was no trace of the accident.

At about 7 a.m. I woke Elena with a full breakfast and a thousand apologies. I remember her giving me a passionate kiss to console me.

It was probably the most embarrassing situation I've ever experienced: shitting myself in a woman's bed the first night I spent with her! But the important thing – for the purposes of this chapter, at least – is that, despite everything, it didn't matter! Elena and I were together for several years; we loved each other very much, and we always laughed when we remembered the incident.

At the time, I was still easily embarrassed. But, thanks to cognitive therapy, it's history. Over the years – and with plenty of rational exercises – I've become totally shameless: I give hundreds of talks in Spain and abroad, I appear on television shows, and I don't feel any tension. But that's not all: I lead the life I want to lead, hold beliefs that many people fiercely criticize, and I don't care.

Freeing myself from the fear of ridicule has made me a much freer person, and shyness has simply disappeared from my personality. I know that we can all do it.

BEING A YANOMAMI INDIAN

The first argument against shame is that we're all the same, no matter what everyone else says. Everyone: President Obama, the fishmonger in my neighborhood, the cleaning lady, the Pope, Bin Laden, any destitute person... We all have exactly the same value: we're precious because we're people. This belief is key when it comes to losing our embarrassment. We must not overlook it. We must explore it as deeply as possible.

The Amazon's Yanomami Indians – a human group of particular interest to me because they live naturally and they're happy – have no chiefs and consider everyone to have the same status. In reality, under our suits and ties, we are all as naked as the Yanomami. Our bodies are similar. We have the same basic preoccupations and live in the same universe, which, by the way, we know nothing about. Under the Pope's white cassock, there is a man who, in the jungle, would reveal himself to be like everyone else. That is the essence of all of us. And the day we regain our sanity and return to natural life, things will become clear at a stroke.

Being skillful, clever, outgoing, elegant, beautiful, rich, or whatever... does not make us any different because, in reality, in the most basic way of life – that is, surviving in the wild – we're all equal. Gaining a deep understanding of this fact crushes our fear of being less, no matter how many mistakes we make. Obama, the Pope, Mother Teresa, Rafa Nadal... they shit themselves, too, when some Indian food disagrees with them. No one is more than anyone else – ever! Whatever happens.

DISREGARDING TRIVIAL QUALITIES

The second big principle for banishing shame is that the only important value is our capacity to love life and others. Intelligence counts for nothing when it comes to being happy, nor does beauty or talents of any kind. I have met very intelligent people – brilliant mathematicians, for instance – who are very unhappy and many beautiful young women who are suicidal. None of that is of the slightest value.

An intense love of life, unrestrained joy and love are priceless, on the other hand, because they bring happiness. What does it matter if we fail, make mistakes, lack skills or certain qualities... if none of that brings fulfillment?

I must stress that, to lose our shame, we must accept these beliefs profoundly. We can only be free from the fear of making fools of ourselves if we do so through to the core of our minds.

Not long ago, I was lucky enough to be invited to give a talk to some people I greatly admire: Alcoholics Anonymous members. They were celebrating the eighteenth anniversary since their founding, and I was able to meet an exceptional group of people of all ages – young and old – and all professions – journalists, lawyers, judges, etc. And almost all of them had an inner joy, the twinkle in their eyes typical of someone who has discovered a new, fuller way of living. These people had come back from hell and were now living very close to heaven.

RADICAL HUMILITY

One of the steps in the Alcoholics Anonymous method is to develop radical humility, which is an essential virtue for becoming a strong person, not just for alcoholics but for everyone. In fact, I am convinced that whenever we lose our way it is to a large extent due to the opposite: because of arrogance, thinking too highly of ourselves. But we can regain our sanity as soon as we stop wanting to be important.

It's not for nothing that madmen have always been caricatured with a paper cone as a hat and a hand on their chest, imitating Napoleon. And it's true that psychotics often have delusions of grandeur. Their need for notoriety is such that it is not enough for them to believe that they are company directors or good artists. They have to be much more than that: Jesus Christ! Or God Himself! They don't realise that there's nothing worse than being so important. How stressful it is to have so much responsibility! Besides, being so notable sets us apart from others.

I don't want to be anything like that. On the contrary, I want to be an everyday person, someone like a shepherd, as my father was in his youth. Just one more member of the group, able to be a friend to others, to take them by the shoulder and go for a walk in the countryside. Because power – or fame – is a curse that makes people lonely and sad. Equality, on the other hand, is loving and participatory.

Alcoholics Anonymous, which has almost a hundred years of experience healing millions of people, says that the true cause of the disease of severe alcoholism is arrogance. A superiority complex makes us so weak that we need to get drunk every day. The disaster that thinking too much of oneself brings about is such that they have to drink to endure life.

To heal, the first thing they have to do is stop wanting to be special. But radically! They have to shun prizes, recognition, medals, and adornments. Alcoholics Anonymous members must focus on mutual collaboration and love. This is why they begin their discussions in their meetings by saying, for example, "My name is James, and I'm an alcoholic." The purpose of this sentence is to wash oneself down with humility. There's nothing better for the mind! From there, personal growth begins.

EXTRASENSORY POWERS

A rather unusual person once came to see me at the practice. She was a fifty-something woman named Pepa, who was a fan of my work.

"I've read your books, and I love them! I trust you. I think you're the only person who can help me," she said.

"Go on," I replied.

"I hear voices. But I'm not crazy. I know that they're spirits that guide my life."

As soon as Pepa entered my office, I guessed she could have psychosis, the diagnostic label ascribed to people who experience hallucinations or delusions. Her physical appearance betrayed her. Schizophrenics often dress sloppily; they're disheveled and lack empathy when they communicate – they're absorbed in their own world.

In response to her assertion, I asked her, "And do these voices bother you?"

"They usually help me, but sometimes they say nasty things. That's why I want you to help me: I want to control them, master this power."

I decided to go straight to the point, and after hearing her whole story, I said, "Don't be angry with me because I'm going to be honest. In my opinion, you have a disease that makes you hear these voices even though they don't exist. Human beings can experience hallucinations under hypnosis, for instance. But there's nothing real in it. I can help you to stop hearing them but not to 'use the power' because they're not real."

Pepa looked very serious but suddenly gave a wry smile.

"I thought you were different, but I see you're not. You're just like the psychiatrists who visited me. You don't have the sensitivity to understand me," she told me.

"I'm going to tell you the truth, Pepa. Please, don't be upset; I think it will do you good. I think you have a very big superiority complex."

"Me? What're you talking about? I'm a very humble person. That's you, showing off your degrees and thinking you're a big shot. Like the psychiatrists!"

"Pepa, I studied hard, and nothing I say is my own invention. All I do is explain what others have discovered. The degrees tell you I've been trained to use certain methods, like thousands of psychologists all over the world. But you'll notice that I don't have the 'honor' of being chosen by spirits for private communication. That's a very lofty thing, don't you think?" I suggested in the most delicate tone I could.

"It's a matter of sensitivity. That's all. It's something you're born with," she explained.

"Sure, Pepa. But it just so happens that this power places you in a position of incredible superiority. You're a chosen one! And I think that's your real problem: you think too much of yourself. I can assure you that to be happy, it is much better to not want to be special."

Over the years, I've seen quite a few cases of schizophrenia, and all of them had in common an exacerbated desire to be center stage: they believed themselves to have powers, special sensitivities, and vital missions to save the world. But as I said before, wanting to be that important comes with a huge burden that will drive anyone crazy.

GOING DOWN TO CLIMB TO THE TOP

In all my books, I've discussed the concept of *going down to climb to the top,* and it's a way of putting radical humility into practice. It involves finding the pleasure in going down, letting go of qualities, and being less – with our heads held high – because beauty, intelligence, extroversion, etc., no longer interests us. Now, we go all in on love to feel renewed, full of energy, and self-confident. There's no better self-esteem than the kind that's based on radical humility! *Going down to climb to the top* is about being able to say to someone who belittles you for being ugly or foolish, "Whatever. I don't need to be handsome or smart anymore. They're qualities that weak people value. If you need them, you're on the wrong path." And to not bat an eyelid. Going down takes us to the top because it makes us more mature, above what others might think about rubbish attributes.

The strategy of going down removes our fear of ridicule because we're prepared for others to think what they want of us. Our self-esteem is firmly set on our loving qualities, and we know that they're wrong to value intelligence or beauty. Self-esteem based on our capacity to love is immovable. The kind that's based on false qualities is always shaky because the day that we're recognized as clever or beautiful, we're satisfied, and the day we're not, we go downhill.

Whenever we have a thought or an emotion related to ridicule, we can think, "I can go to the bottom and be happy. I don't need things to be right. I just need to love." If we find ourselves feeling afraid that we'll do a bad presentation, for example, we can say, "I could be the worst speaker on the planet, and I couldn't care less!"

BEING A DOG

Diogenes was one of the great philosophers of Greece – the greatest, perhaps – and his reputation was based on his way of life.

This long-bearded man chose to live in poverty, rejecting his family's wealth.

But at the beginning of his career, all of Athens was shocked when he decided to live in a barrel. He asked a wine merchant friend for one of his gigantic casks, laid it down by the steps to the agora, and made it his home. Satisfied, Diogenes slept there and used it to store his meager belongings.

In those first days living in the barrel, one of his best friends, Lucian, a childhood companion, asked him, "Is it really necessary for you to live like this? Aren't you overdoing it?"

"It's just an experiment, Lucian. I've lived as a noble. Now I have to show that I can be happy as a beggar," the philosopher concluded.

But what Athens understood least was why he adopted such a strange nickname. Shortly after moving into the barrel, he wanted people to call him "the Dog", and from then on, his followers would be "dogs" like him. Diogenes himself explained why:

"From now on, I am 'Diogenes the Dog' because, like an animal, I want to practice a wonderful skill: not caring about the opinions of others. Dogs are free to do whatever they want, and they are never embarrassed. So let us be known as the *cynoi* – the dogs – and our philosophy, the *cynica*."

I love the nickname "the Dog" because to free ourselves from shame, we must be a *cynos*, someone who knows that what we need to be happy is within ourselves, and this autonomy is an asset that must be protected from the flawed opinions of others.

PISSING ON OUR CRITICS

They say that Diogenes was once invited to a wealthy admirer's banquet. At one of the tables sat Erasthenes, a rival philosopher who was preceptor to most of Athens's rich kids and enjoyed a very high status. Even so, he was envious and could not bear to be seen as a simple teacher, while Diogenes was considered a wise man, a living legend.

At one point, Erasthenes, spurred on by drink, raised his hand and threw a bone to Diogenes, saying, "There you go, Dog, succulent food!"

Diogenes, also inflamed by the wine, stood and went over to the teacher's group. Everyone fell silent to hear his witty retort, but he merely rolled up his robe and lifted his leg to let out a fierce stream of urine. Laughter broke out in the room, and Diogenes raised his voice to conclude, "Indeed, I can eat bones and urinate on so-called sages as a dog would. Don't lose heart, friend. Perhaps one day you will also be able to."

FEAR OF BLUSHING

Some people are afraid of blushing, so much so that they cause the problem by flushing red from their own nerves. The solution, of course, lies precisely in not attaching any importance to the issue and telling oneself, "If I turn red, it doesn't matter. If people realize something is making me nervous, then let them know. And if they think I'm weak, that's their problem! No one is weak because they blush. The value of people lies only in our capacity to love!"

In Japan, this fear reaches unimaginable extremes. Many people never leave their homes because of it.

How ridiculous! We all blush from time to time! And if it happened to us all day long, incurably, it wouldn't matter!

Speaking in public and it goes badly – who cares? We're all worth exactly the same.

Trying to flirt and we get rejected – so what? It even happens to George Clooney.

Stumbling and falling to the ground in a fancy restaurant – there could be nothing more human!

Is there anyone these things never happen to? Let's be *cynoi*, let's be Yanomami Indians, let's be people who love, above all else. There's nothing greater than wanting to be just another person.

In this chapter we learned that:

1. Shame is overcome by realising that:
 a. We're all worth the same.
 b. The only valuable quality is our capacity to love.
2. The key to strong self-esteem is radical humility.
3. The most elevated people are, paradoxically, those who have no problem "going down".
4. Let's accept as soon as possible that we will be criticised and adopt the nickname *cynoí*.

12
Getting Rid of Bad Habits

A very devout man went to Mass every day and followed all the rules of the Church. One day, there was a flood, and the streets and houses of his city were submerged. The man went up onto the roof of his home, but the water level kept rising. Up there, on his knees, he asked God for help.

Before long, a military boat appeared. A soldier offered to take him on board.

"No, thanks. God will save me," said the devout man.

Soon after, the water reached the roof, and he was forced to start swimming. After an hour, another boat passed by. This time, they threw him a life jacket, but he refused it.

"No, thanks. God will save me," he yelled from the water.

At the end of the day, a helicopter with a powerful searchlight found him still swimming, exhausted now. They immediately threw him a rope to rescue him.

"No, thanks. God will... glug, glug, glug."

The devout man spent, sank, and disappeared into the water. When he woke up, he was before God.

"Lord, you said you would save me, but you let me die!" he cried discontented.

"I tried," God said, "but you spurned my help."

"I did not!" said the devout man.

"Listen to me," God explained. "I sent you a boat, a life jacket, and even a helicopter! If that's not help, I don't know what is!"

Paula had a habit of practicing compulsive sex. She was a very beautiful and intelligent woman, a doctor, and she made the most of the fact that she was single by frolicking every day with one of her many friends with benefits. Sometimes, she did so with two different men on the same day. But, she told me, with many of them, she didn't enjoy it. She saw it more as something mundane; when the men left her house, she was free – alone at last! But she preferred this compulsive entertainment to the dizziness of not having anything to do.

In our first sessions, she admitted,

"I don't know why I do it! I realize it's a compulsion, like binge eating."

"I think I do know, Paula. You do it because, on those nights, you feel like you need the distraction of sex. If you don't have that adventure, you feel empty. You have a typical fear of inactivity," I pointed out.

"You're right! That's the exact feeling I get! If one of my dates doesn't show up, I have to quickly find another in my address book because I feel like something's wrong," she admitted. "But how can I overcome it?"

"By thinking in the right way. I'll teach you."

We've all been swept away by the force of a harmful habit, like eating junk food, hanging around with people who aren't good for us, or playing video games instead of doing something productive. We say that they're compulsive when we do these things to fill a neurotic void – or, in other words, a void that doesn't exist.

Void-filling habits prevent us from leading a truly enthralling life because these behaviors – compulsive as they are – end up grey, "mundane," as Paula put it, more an obligation than something that is chosen freely. They can often cause serious problems, like pathological gambling, risky sex, or unhealthy weight gain.

And the truth is that almost everyone has some bad habits of this kind, even if they're minor. Let's see how to get rid of them once and for all.

TOUCHING THE STONE OF POWER

In one Indiana Jones movie, the intrepid professor goes in search of some stones that grant enormous power. Whip in hand, he explores the jungle and bravely risks his life. The prize was worth it. Paula and I also went in search of the "stones of power." Unlike Indy's, ours were real and granted emotional strength and a sweet, exciting, fulfilling life. And just by touching them, harmful habits would be eliminated.

The stone of emotional power represents a *deep love of life*. To activate it, we must ALWAYS focus on the joy of doing EVERYTHING with passion, including the little things simple everyday activities.

People who feel the need to do void-filling activities must reject them as soon as they feel the compulsion, commit to a fuller life, and gear themselves toward having a passion for the little things. The following outline shows the process to follow:

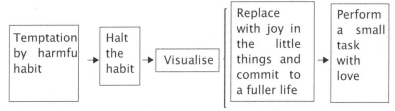

The penultimate double step is the most important one: *Replace with joy in the little things* alongside *Commit to a fuller life*. To complete this step, my patients perform a meditation/visualisation that can be done while walking and listening to music. I detail this *visualization of a full life* in my book *Las gafas de la felicidad* ("*The Happiness Glasses*").

The aim is to persuade oneself – through visualization – that we can learn to enjoy each of the nine areas of our lives to extremes that we never imagined: working with passion, loving our families, exercising, leisure, friendship, spirituality, learning, and partners.

In our imagination, we see ourselves enjoying every small thing because we pay attention to what we have in hand. We make the most of all of our facets! We resolve to lead great lives! This is the real stone of power in life: learning to get excited about everything.

Wherever the stone of power is, may our gloomy compulsions be banished!

In this visualization, there is a moment when we can see ourselves with a photo album in our hands. We show it to someone and explain the life we have: What delightful family relationships! What a life of leisure in the mountains, by the sea, at the cinema, or in concert halls! How we enjoy our work!

My patients learn to "visualize a full life" whenever a compulsive habit comes into their heads. Then, they take a second step: choosing a task to perform with joy. These two activities – visualization and performing a small task – effectively replace any impulse they have. Guaranteed! This simple two-step maneuver eliminates the feeling of emptiness and allows us to discover a whole host of much more constructive habits.

GLORIOUS SUNDAY AFTERNOONS

In my book *Las Gafas de la Felicidad,* I also talked about the Sunday afternoon blues, a low mood common all over the world, which is essentially a bad feeling that sets in when the weekend is over because it seems like there's nothing left to do like something has died.

I sometimes experienced it when I was young, but for many years, it has been more than buried. People who suffer from it do so because they feel this absurd emptiness, this fear of doing nothing. The same fear that awakens harmful habits like compulsive sex or gambling.

Nowadays, my Sunday afternoons are glorious, one of my favorite parts of the week. I usually stay at home, make myself a nice cup of tea, and tune in to my favorite radio channel. With this fantastic backdrop, I turn on my computer and choose a task I feel like doing. It's often a mechanical job like organizing files or replying to emails, but I do it while thoroughly enjoying the moment: steaming tea, good music, and sweet, constructive work. Besides my computer, I always have a pen and paper to note down the titles of the songs I discover on the radio program. Then I search for them on Spotify and add them to my music library.

After about forty-five minutes, I take a well-deserved break to distract my mind: I check Facebook, write a nice WhatsApp message to a friend, or go out for a short walk. My Sunday afternoons are delightful and rewarding. The total opposite of the absurd emptiness that leads to a compulsive habit. The secret is to learn that every single moment of our lives can be glorious. All we need to do is put love and passion into the present, appreciate small tasks, and realize that it's up to us to make them *glorious*.

A FULLER LIFE

The main motivation for getting rid of negative habits is the knowledge that, by eliminating them, we move closer to a much fuller life if we give up our void-filling activities to nourish a love of life – in a big way! – we will head in a great direction. That's what Paula did. It was easy for her to give up mindless sex once she realized that she could replace it with something far better: being much happier in general, filling her life only with meaningful acts that propel her towards fulfillment. Always working towards a sweet, intensely beautiful life!

Every night, when she arrived home, she thought, "I'm going to have a wonderful, interesting, fulfilling life. And I can do it right now by doing a small task with love." And for ten minutes she visualised herself in what would be her new life of confidence and strength. Within a few weeks, she had forgotten her compulsion. It was that easy.

The following outline once again summarises the two steps to ending unhelpful habits:

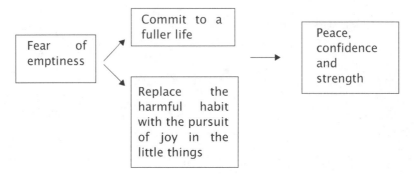

AN EXCITING LIFE, ALWAYS

Another patient, a very intelligent ten-year-old boy, said to me, "Sometimes I feel bad because I wish I lived in the Harry Potter world. I would love to live in England, at a school for wizards. And when I see I'm here in Barcelona, I feel sad."

And not infrequently, people ask me, "Rafael, isn't life boring once you grow up? Because you've discovered everything, and all that's left is repetition and tedium."

To all those who think that adult life is monotonous, I reply that this is only because they are convinced of it. And it prevents them from being excited by what they have in hand. The reality is that the older we are, the MORE opportunities there are to enjoy ourselves.

To give just one example: as a child and young person, I had no idea how incredible work, learning, and study could be. I was only able to acquire this intense enjoyment as an adult because only now is my mind capable of appreciating my opportunities and the wonders of a fleeting life.

If we get excited about our tasks, as small as they may be, if we set stimulating goals for ourselves and small challenges, and if we do things with love, life becomes a wonderful adventure, anywhere and forever! As wonderful as you make it!

I haven't had "pastimes" in years. I never just pass the time because my life is full of exciting tasks: things to do with love that contribute to my happiness. I kick back and have fun, of course, but it's not about killing time; it's to gather my strength to return to my exciting life. I enjoy myself much more now than when I was a boy or young man because I know a lot of ways to live life with love!

Boredom has also disappeared from my life. When I travel by train or plane, for instance, in the waiting rooms, I usually spend the time in front of my laptop absorbed in something interesting. I put on my headphones with my favorite music, a coffee to one side and have a fantastic time waiting! Traveling is exciting, even during changeovers!

Any moment can be glorious if we focus with enthusiasm on loving life and the various tasks that can brighten it. We don't need bad habits because there's no void to fill. Life is always full.

In this chapter we learned:

1. Void-filling habits seek to fill an absurd inner void, which is a fear of doing nothing, of being bored.
2. There are two steps to breaking these habits:
   a. Being ambitious and wanting to lead a very sweet and intense life.
   b. Performing small tasks with love.

13
Learning to Do Nothing

Why have we lost our ability to be idle? How often do we sit down serenely without doing anything at all, with no purpose or destination, firmly planted in the present, free?

Henry D. Thoreau

Mullah Nasreddin was in his garden. He had been working in the orchard all morning, and he sat in the shade to cool off.

Observing a beautiful pumpkin, he thought, "Allah, your wisdom is great, but there are some things I would have done differently. Look at this impressive pumpkin that grows on the ground. And then look at the walnut: a little thing that grows hanging from a majestic tree. I would have done it the other way around: glorious pumpkins would hang from magnificent trees, and walnuts would come out of the earth."

And he sat there for a while, smug, imagining other creations. A gentle breeze blew the branches overhead. At once, a walnut fell onto the mullah's round bald patch with a sharp thud. Nasreddin let out a scream, and a bump immediately formed on his head. But then, in that very place, he decided to prostrate himself before God. Smiling, he said, "Oh Allah, forgive me. Your wisdom is truly great. If it had been me who had arranged things on Earth, I would not be praying to you now but in the hospital, broken by the impact of a pumpkin.

One of the most common neuroses these days is a fear of doing nothing, of being at a loose end. The ominous void of inactivity. Some people struggle when they find themselves with nothing to do, especially at a time when they "should" be working or making the most of the time. A feeling of guilt, of uselessness, then adds to the discomfort. As a result of this neurosis, many people prefer to fill all their time with various obligations or tasks.

The musician Joaquín Sabina once admitted that he had this problem, which I call "idlephobia" or a fear of inactivity. Sabina said that he self-imposed an obligation to work every day, so he would sit at the desk and write poems or songs. If he didn't, he felt a depressing void, guilt, even disorientation.

The number of severe idlephobes is lower than 1% of the population, but nowadays, we all suffer from this fear a little. As Thoreau said in the quote at the head of this chapter, we have lost our ability to be idle. In any case, it's a neurosis that we would all do well to overcome because it's a fear that prevents us from relaxing completely. It also stops us from freely choosing what we want to do in life. This fear, however slight, makes us go too fast and enslaves us.

I once had a patient whom we'll call Rosa, a civil servant in her fifties. She worked from 8 a.m. to 3 p.m. on fairly routine tasks, but in the office, she felt fine and calm. When she returned home in the afternoon, the discomfort began: she felt a great neurotic void, and the hours dragged on until nightfall. Then she went to bed, a nervous wreck.

Until a year ago, she'd filled her free time with exercise, attending courses at community centers, and meeting her best friend, but now she had an injury that prevented her from going to the gym. She'd had enough of the courses, and had argued with her soul mate. She was haunted by the ghost of inactivity!

Patients with a fear of doing nothing often have a particularly hard time on holiday. And when they travel, they tend to visit places in a hurry, filling all their time with the contents of the most detailed travel guide.

Many people with addictions owe their problem to idlephobia and turn to drinking, pathological gambling, or compulsive sex to block out the threat of the inactivity void. Their fear is such that they throw themselves into harmful activities like playing slot machines, which in reality are much more boring and monotonous than total inactivity itself. I remember another patient, a 35-year-old Englishwoman, a mother and housewife, who went around with a thick notebook full of to-do lists, gnawed by continuous use. She would arrive at the practice with her tongue hanging out and leave just as hurriedly in pursuit of more and more activity. She was thin, and her body was always tense. Her life was a constant flight from the ghost of inactivity.

BEING INACTIVE ALL OUR LIVES

We're going to learn here that we could be completely inactive all our lives and have a great time. And not only that but there is the paradox that, in activity, we could produce some of the most valuable assets for society, namely artistic creations and expressions of spirituality.

No one *needs* to be active, whether on days off or working days. There are many reasons why we could be perfectly happy in a state of complete idleness:

a) Because it's the natural state of the human being.

b) Because many people are happy doing nothing, and they're not extraterrestrials. In other words, it's possible.

c) Because if there's one thing the planet needs, it's some inactivity instead of so much neurotic work that ravages the environment.

d) Because it's in sweet idleness, when the mind wanders, that great ideas arise – scientific or artistic.

With these and other arguments, when we've fully convinced ourselves that we don't need to do anything, we will banish our fear of inactivity and benefit from it hugely. First, we'll choose what we want to do in every moment of our lives without compulsions that block out neurotic discomfort. Then we'll work at a much more pleasant pace, like Buddhist monks, who do little but do it beautifully.

And finally, we'll be more creative because good ideas only emerge from peace of mind.

WHAT'S GOOD IS WHAT'S NATURAL

From a young age, I've been interested in anthropology. It's a fascinating discipline that seeks to explain why human beings live in the way they do and what causes their moral differences. Why are we so in favour of monogamy? Why do we live in father and mother families and not in larger groups? Are there more harmonious ways to live? Anthropology calls into question our customs by comparing us to other peoples and times.

Reading the great anthropologists, I notice that almost all of them are fascinated by "acculturated" tribal groups, to the point that they assert that they have discovered true happiness in them. It happened with the researchers who studied the natives of Polynesia, those who lived with the Eskimos of the North Pole, with American Indians, African Pygmies, Australian Aboriginals... with all of them! And I don't know exactly why, but I took a liking to one of these people: the Yanomami of the Amazon. Perhaps it was after seeing a TVE documentary as a boy, *Otros pueblos* ("Other Peoples") by the journalist Luis Pancorbo (available on the TVE website).

But what's relevant to the issue of idlephobia is the fact that these tribal peoples never suffer from this fear. The Yanomami Indians only work an hour a day. They get up early and go out in search of food – hunting and gathering – before the sun starts beating down. And in that time, they obtain everything they need. What do they do for the rest of the day? Very important tasks: visiting other tribes, talking, educating children with love, playing, and, above all, craftwork. For example, they polish a wooden bow with great skill or carefully fasten the eaves of their large communal huts – an ancestral do-it-yourself that fills them with harmonious joy.

For many historians, anthropologists, economists, and psychologists, the natural state of the human being is to work very little. *Homo sapiens* is like a lion: hunts once a week, gorge on meat, and spends the rest of the time frolicking in the sun, majestic and happy. Let's face it: our pace has never been like the frenetic ants.

If we become aware of this, we realize that what's natural is to spend much more time strolling, contemplating nature, wandering, talking... constantly, every day.

Where does that leave our absurd need to always be busy? In the dustbin of irrational beliefs, of course.

To lend weight to this idea, I think it's worth mentioning the Englishman Stuart Mill, one of the first great economists. In around 1850, at the beginning of the madness of mass production, he wondered, "Towards what ultimate point is society tending by its industrial progress? When the progress ceases, in what condition are we to expect that it will leave mankind?"

As we will see in more detail, we have been sold the idea that material progress is the panacea of happiness, and that's why we must always be busy. But only two hundred years after the beginning of the industrial era have we realized that we have been wrong. Now, we could answer Stuart Mill by saying, "Industrial progress leads to the destruction of the planet in more ways than you could ever imagine: the erosion of the ozone layer, the deterioration of the soil and seas, the development of weapons."

The environment is crying out for us to stop producing so many goods, exploiting the planet, polluting the air... In other words, it's imploring us to spend more time quietly doing nothing. So, where does that leave the supposed virtue of extreme effort? In the rubbish dump of total nonsense.

WISDOM AND BEAUTY VERSUS HYSTERICAL FRENZY

One of the figures I most admire is the ingenious British mathematician, logician, philosopher, writer, and Nobel laureate Bertrand Russell. In the early twentieth century, he was an active supporter of women's suffrage and proposed laws in favor of divorce and sex education at a time when it was a mortal sin. At the University of Cambridge, a statue commemorates him as one of the great professors of that wonderful institution.

Russell wrote a book entitled *In Praise of Idleness* where he explains that capitalism has made slaves of us. Indeed, with its dirty factories, the Industrial Revolution brought with it a perverse work ethic. But it didn't used to be like this. Artisans and farmers of antiquity and the Middle Ages had enormous amounts of free time. In ancient Egypt, for example, the religion forbade working for a fifth of the year's days. In classical Greece, summer holidays lasted more than sixty days. And in medieval Europe, with the old Roman calendar, there were 108 days when no one worked for religious reasons – not even the inquisitors!

But the Industrial Revolution changed everything. The company owners imposed a different mindset. In 1820, John Foster, one of the industrial philosophers in the pay of the new owners, said in outrage, "After work, farmers have too much free time! We often see them sitting on a bench or lying by the river, given up to complete lethargy." John Foster was a pioneer of idlephobia.

Along the same lines, the famous nineteenth-century essayist Thomas Carlyle wrote, "Man was created to work, not to speculate, or feel, or dream. Every idle moment is treason." This absurd idea that anything other than work is time wasted seeped into us until it became our minds' second skin.

In Victorian times, many self-help manuals were published urging people to believe that work was the panacea for happiness. *Saving* (1875), *Duty* (1880), or the insane *Early Rising* (1830) were all aimed at persuading people that fourteen-hour shifts in the factory were the rational thing to do. Take these verses that the hysterical Hannah More spewed out precisely in *Early Rising*:

Happiness Declassified

Thou silent murderer, Sloth, no more My mind imprison'd keep; Nor let me waste another hour With thee, thou felon Sleep.

The renowned Methodist John Wesley got up every day at four in the morning and wrote the sermon *The Duty and Advantage of Early Rising* (1786), which is priceless:

By soaking so long between warm sheets, the flesh is as it were par-boiled and becomes soft and flabby. The nerves, in the meantime, are quite unstrung.

Wesley was undoubtedly another champion of neurosis.

In the face of so much industrial madness, I would pay more attention to Jesus Christ, who withdrew to the desert for forty days to connect with God. A good sabbatical! (Incidentally, Christ had no known trade). Or Buddha, who spent several years sitting under a tree meditating.

In the East and in the West, holy men who devote themselves to doing nothing have always been valued. *Sadhus* are wandering mendicants in India who live on alms (and never refuse a joint from young European tourists). Christian hermits disappear into forests or deserts to find total peace. Silence or contemplation are spiritual practices present in every religious tradition. In other words, doing nothing – not even speaking – is an exercise that elevates the spirit, that refines our spirituality.

The American writer Ernest Hemingway wrote for just one hour a day. He said it was his key to producing sublime texts. By limiting his workload, he ensured he always felt passionate about writing. Because working less distills the best of us, it stimulates art and truly elevated activities.

VISUALISING INACTIVITY

To free ourselves of idlephobia, I recommend *visualizing pleasant inactivity*. This consists of imagining ourselves feeling perfectly happy doing nothing, picturing ourselves being inactive for long periods of time for our entire lives, perhaps.

I visualize myself as a relaxed traveler backpacking around the world: observing, mentally wandering, writing, and painting in my travel journal. Good travellers can be in the most inhospitable or boring location and have a great time because they are able to appreciate the beauty of each place. There are beautiful things everywhere, interesting experiences to recount in one of those early twentieth-century moleskin notebooks.

When I visualize pleasant inactivity, I can see myself as one of these traveler-poets in my neighborhood, in my day-to-day. This allows me to swim with the current, calmly contemplating my surroundings to translate them into poetry.

I see myself as the tramp who picks up a discarded newspaper and reads a well-written report, appreciating it for the treasure that it is. These pleasures are ineffable priceless, and I access them thanks to my state of mind, which flows with the present, without obligations, in peace.

And I imagine myself being able to meditate or pray for entire days, months, or years. And I calm my mind like a monk in a monastery. I connect with God or with nature. I don't need to produce anything, and an abundance of beauty comes to me.

I'm like the painter of everyday scenes who finds the sublime in any image that passes in front of him. Like Edward Hopper in his painting *Nighthawks*: four people sitting in a café at night. Time stops, and we understand that, in some way, we are eternal.

Then I will be like what the poet John Keats described in this 1830 text:

> *I had an idea that a Man might pass a very pleasant life in this manner – Let him on a certain day read a certain page of full Poesy or distilled Prose, and let him wander upon it, and bring home to it, and prophesy upon it, and dream upon it... How happy is such a voyage of concentration? What delicious diligent Indolence!*

It is nobler to be seated like Jupiter than to fly like Mercury; let's not rush around everywhere collecting like bees, buzzing impatiently wherever we go, knowing everything in advance; instead, let's allow our petals to open like a flower's and be passive and receptive.

We can all become fully free and calm beings. People who choose what they want to do and create beauty wherever they go. It will make us heroes like Mingliaotse, the wandering Taoist monk of the seventeenth century who said in one of his poems,

I walk along the sandy shore, where there are golden clouds and crystal waters;

the fairies' mastiffs bark in surprise... I go in and lose myself in the pear tree.

And finally, one of my favorite poems, by Miguel Hernández, another champion of rationality:

SOLITUDE

In this autumn siesta, under this colossal elm, whose round leaves it has already

begun to cast into the wind, you give me full, sweet, and lone Solitude.

Just one bird, the one of all my siestas, taps on the elm, its musical trill quick,

as if in a hurry to finish.

How I love you!

How grateful I am to you for coming to give me,

in this autumn siesta, under this colossal elm, such sweet, such full and such lone Solitude!

In this chapter we learned that:

1. Fear of doing nothing prevents us from completely relaxing and freely choosing what we want to do; it also makes us hurry and enslaves us.

2. Idlephobia is the main cause of addictions.

3. The natural state of the human being is not work, but idleness. We can all be happy without doing anything at all.

4. The planet needs a little inactivity, instead of so much neurotic work that depletes the environment.

5. It's from sweet idleness that great ideas arise – scientific or artistic.

14
Stabler Moods

In a Chinese village lived a farmer with his son. They were humble, and apart from their land, their only possession was a horse. One ill-fated day, the animal ran away and left the man with no motive or power with which to plow the land. When his neighbors came to comfort him, he thanked them for a visit and asked, "How can you know it was a misfortune?"

Everyone was surprised by his comment, and when they left, they said in low voices, "He doesn't want to accept reality. Let him think what he wants if it stops him feeling sad."

A week later, the horse returned to the stable, but he didn't return alone: he brought a beautiful mare with him for company.

When they found out, everyone understood the farmer's reaction.

They went to visit him and congratulated him on his good fortune: "You only had one horse. Now you have two. Congratulations!"

"Thank you very much for your words," the farmer replied. "But how can you know that it is a blessing?"

This time, they thought he had gone mad: "Does he not see that God has sent him a gift?"

Soon after, the farmer's son decided to train the mare, but the animal leaped unexpectedly and struck the boy, breaking his leg.

Happiness Declassified

The neighbors went to see the farmer again. The mayor solemnly declared that everyone was very sad about what had happened.

The man thanked him for his kindness but asked, "How can you know that what happened was a misfortune?"

Everyone was stunned because nobody doubted that an injured son was a tragedy. When they left the farmer's house, they said to each other, "This man is in a really bad way! His only son might be left lame, and still he doubts that what happened is an adversity."

After a few weeks, Japan declared war on China, and the army conscripted all the young men to go to the front. All of them except the farmer's son, who had a broken leg. None of the boys from the area came home alive.

Time passed. The two animals had offspring that yielded good money and, better still, the son recovered. The farmer visited his neighbors often to comfort and help them because they had always been supportive.

Whenever someone complained, the farmer would say, "How do you know this is a misfortune?"

And if someone was very happy, he would ask, "How do you know this is a blessing?"

And the people of that village understood that, beyond appearances, life has many meanings.

I once had a fourteen-year-old patient, Carol, who was a delight: kind, intelligent, and creative. Despite her young age, she was an excellent violinist. But dark bouts of depression were blackening her life. The same disease that Winston Churchill called "my black dog."

Carol would feel sad for no reason. The sadness would simply appear and grip her for an afternoon or two until it went away by itself. When there was a reason, it was usually a minor thing, like getting bored in a museum.

"Why is this happening to me?" she asked in our first session, looking at me with her beautiful dark eyes. Her mother thought it could be due to her recent separation or perhaps a neurochemical deficiency, but she was wrong in both cases.

In this chapter, we will examine how spontaneous depression or anxiety occurs and how we can overcome it to cultivate a stable mood, allowing us to always be cheerful and full of energy.

From a psychological perspective, short-term depression works in the same way as anxiety or any psychosomatic illness: fibromyalgia, chronic fatigue, psychological stomach pain, or headaches. They're what I call *pseudophysical complaints*. They appear to have been caused by a medical condition – a virus, a neuronal problem, etc. – but in reality, they originate in the mind.

WHY DO I GET DEPRESSED?

The first psychotherapy session with Carol consisted of explaining in detail why she had these low moods. Understanding them was critical to her therapy.

"All this happens for a pretty silly reason: you get depressed because you're afraid of getting depressed," I said.

"Afraid of getting depressed? I don't think so! I'm so happy in the morning, and in the afternoon, I suddenly feel down," she answered back.

"Carol, even if you don't perceive it directly, you *are* afraid. When you feel sad, in the first few seconds, your mind tells you, *Oh no, there it is again. I have to get rid of it!* And then your efforts to banish it in those first few seconds make you feel worse," I explained.

"It's just that these lows really are a nightmare!" she said gloomily. "You know?"

"You're going to learn to prevent these low moods by eliminating your initial fear: mentally accepting that you could have them forever and still be very happy. With this mental exercise, they'll disappear, trust me," I concluded.

Another of my patients, Miguel, was a forty-year-old guy who owned a very successful small chain of greengrocers. Life was going very well for him; he had a partner and a great passion for mountain biking. But an emotional problem plagued him. He was irritable and anxious and didn't know why.

"Most days, I get up feeling on edge, and as the day goes on, I get more and more anxious. By the evening, I can't bear it anymore. I went to a neurologist, but he told me I don't have any kind of disorder or vitamin deficiency," he explained to me.

"Are there ever days when you're free of it?" I asked.

"Some. And I also don't know why that is. Hence, the doctor thinks it's psychological," he replied.

I saw Miguel for about three months, and in the first sessions, he was so anxious that his voice trembled. It was as if he had some kind of creature inside him that set him on edge and made him tense up.

In fact, this kind of unexplained anxiety or irritability is one of the most common emotional problems. The person wakes up in the morning – or from a nap – with an unpleasant feeling that everything bothers them, with hyperexcitability and frayed nerves. And the worst thing is that nothing is causing it! It's as if the body has triggered the anxiety by releasing a substance in the brain.

Miguel's anxiety and Carol's low moods were two manifestations of the same problem, and the solution was to do the exercise I will explain below.

THE VICIOUS CIRCLE OF FEAR

All psychosomatic symptoms are caused by a *vicious circle of fear*: we experience an unpleasant feeling and stay glued to it,

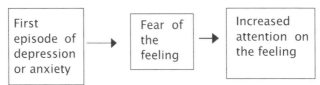

attracting it to ourselves with our attention – we even amplify it until it becomes a problem. If we disregard it from the outset, it dissolves within a few minutes like a slight itch on our arm.

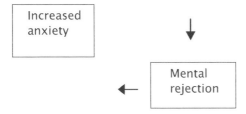

Breaking this circle involves not rejecting the feeling. To achieve this, we must convince ourselves of a premise: "I could be very happy with depression or anxiety." It is what I call *full acceptance of the symptom*.

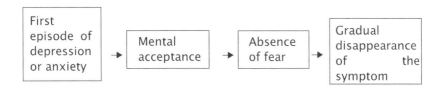

There are many ways to achieve acceptance of the symptom. Let's look at some arguments that will help us. The aim is to stop catastrophizing the problem, to start seeing it as a minor adversity, and even to appreciate its benefits.

"But how can there be anything good about depression?" Carol asked me.

"I assure you, there is, and when you start to perceive it curiously, you'll stop experiencing it," I replied.

THE OLD NOTION OF VIRTUE

Laura once asked her eleven-year-old daughter Alba, "Which part of the body is the most important?"

"The ears, mum," the girl replied.

"Many people are deaf and manage perfectly well. But think about it, and you'll guess," she said affectionately.

Over the next few weeks, the girl reflected, and she thought she'd found a brilliant answer.

"I got it, mum: sight is the most essential sense. So the most important part of the body is the eyes!"

"You're learning quickly, but that's not the right answer. Plenty of blind people are happy even though they can't see," her mother pointed out.

A few months later, the girl's grandfather died. On the day of the funeral, everyone was very sad, and Alba's father cried. The girl was

*moved. Right after the funeral, her mother took her aside and asked,
"Do you know which part of the body is the most important now?"*

"No, mum," the girl replied.

"Today is the best day to tell you. It's the shoulder, my girl."

"Because it holds up your head?" Alba wondered.

*"No. Because your loved ones rest their heads on it when they
cry."*

Two thousand years ago, the Greek philosopher Aristotle preached
that the path to happiness lay in virtue. As a psychologist, I can testify
to this being a great, wonderful, and mind-blowing truth. Although
not the only one, virtue is a very useful way to overcome unexplained
anxiety and depression (or any other psychogenic complaint). Let's
see.

When we experience sadness or anxiety for no reason, a part of
our mind says to itself, "If this carries on, my life is going to be a total
mess!"

And it's true that these symptoms can prevent us from leading a
"normal life." At a romantic dinner, nerves or depression stop us from
being as sweet and as fun as usual. At a concert, we don't have the
strength to dance and enjoy ourselves like everyone else.

It's no surprise, then, that we get the idea that these feelings ruin
our lives. And whether we realize it or not, we wonder, "What can I

do to get rid of this? If I can't, I'm finished!" Then, we look for a way out through distraction, mental struggle, alcohol, or anxiolytics.

I believe that Aristotle, in ancient Athens, experienced these causeless low moods or anxiety, and his search for virtue freed him from them. No doubt, at difficult times, he learned to say to himself, "If I had to remain in this state of mind for my whole life, if there was no way to eliminate it, I would devote myself to others. I would be happy to have a great purpose in life!"

If I had to be depressed forever – something I have thought about already – I would go to live with my friend Jaume Sanllorente in Mumbai, where he runs an orphanage in one of the world's most unequal cities. I would ask him for a room where I could work to raise money for his cause, which would become my own.

I would feel out of sorts and downcast, but I would spend a few hours a day on the project. I would try to pass the rest of the time as peacefully as possible. I would probably try to calm myself down with anxiolytics until the next day. But I'm certain that, every morning, when I opened my window and saw the children playing in the courtyard, their beautiful smiles would be my source of joy, my joyful purpose in life. And that would make me happy.

The cognitive method consists of reasoning that no adversity is bad enough to make us miserable: not death, illness, or loneliness. This is how my admired Stephen Hawking thinks – for him, nothing is terrible. Hawking knows that as long as there is the possibility of doing something beautiful – in his case, high-level scientific research – we can have a purpose in life and ongoing well-being.

In the same way, working with orphaned children in Mumbai, I could be happy despite being depressed. And why not in Barcelona, too? I would choose some other kind of virtue. In fact, why not all of them? There are lots!

Being kind, honest, giving oneself to others, being elegant, creating beauty, cultivating friendship, and being humble are enormous sources of joy. All virtues are fountains of happiness and strength!

Let's look at some of the main virtues that we can cultivate to build emotional strength.

BEING HONEST

Some people have the fixation that life is not interesting enough. They go from home to work and find everything boring. They don't realize that there's a fantastic opportunity for enjoyment in the task of improving themselves as a person. Feeling good inside is always within our reach.

Being honest is about telling the truth even when it hurts. It's about others being able to trust us deeply.

Being very honest is enormously beautiful. Few people are. It involves giving up any advantage or comfort if it means lying or hiding the truth.

GIVING YOURSELF TO OTHERS

The virtue of giving yourself to others is one of the most beautiful, but it's important to understand what it means. It's not about giving material goods – which aren't much help – but warmth, respect, and attention. In other words, friendship.

Because the deepest devotion is in friendship, it's about viewing people as the most beautiful thing in the world and trying to connect with their source of goodness and love.

I remember the first time I experienced profound friendship. I was in year six of primary school, and halfway through the year, I was seated next to Alberto, a boy who'd just arrived in the city; during the months that followed, a lovely bond formed between us. It was the first time I'd felt so happy with a classmate: we helped each other with our homework, explained the little problems to one another, and above all, we had a great time together.

One day, towards the end of the year, he said to me, "You know what, Rafa? You're my best friend!"

At that time, I didn't find it easy to express emotions and I don't think I answered. I just smiled. But I certainly felt the same way. Just the fact that he was there by my side every day made me happier.

Deep friendship is one of the most beautiful experiences, a connection that gives us delightful fulfillment. And we can cultivate it on a daily basis.

THE FUSED COUPLE

One of the most powerful areas of personal growth is in our relationships with partners because they involve perfecting a lot of virtues. And, as we've seen, virtue creates meaning and well-being to the point that it gives us the strength to overcome depression and anxiety.

When we have a condition caused by the mind, we can always think to ourselves, "Okay, I'm hopelessly sad. But if this were to last forever, I could work on my relationship with a special intensity, loving my partner more and better. In this sense, my sadness would spur me on – the more depressed, the more I would concentrate on loving my partner."

So, what kind of relationship would we pursue? What I call a "fused couple."

I once had a very lovely relationship. I won't go into details, but for various reasons we opened ourselves to each other in a very intense way.

We were living in London one ochre-colored autumn, a life of bike rides and books. She was immersed in anthropological research, and I, of course, in my eternal companion, psychology, and we shared texts and discoveries. We spent hours at our favorite coffee shop sprawled on deckchairs, with blankets to keep out the icy breeze. Making love was a very intense experience for us. We really felt like we were inside each other (and we weren't on drugs!).

Being in a fused relationship means having a partner who is your best friend in life. You admire them. And you notice that they feel the same. They are the person you're most comfortable with. You could spend fifteen days lying on a sofa with them without doing anything and feel complete. And this is made possible just by wanting it. It's a matter of opening yourself up to the experience. Love is a function of our mind that we can choose to activate or not. It doesn't depend on circumstances, as we sometimes think, but on ourselves.

Any adversity can become an opportunity to grow through love and cooperation. And when we're sad for no reason, we can cultivate our love for our partner. We can say to ourselves, "I'm depressed, and maybe I will be all my life, but I'll put it to good use by loving my partner more intensely."

THE CURIOUS CURE FOR NEUROSIS

I once met a young Italian woman who lived in Barcelona. She was unusually beautiful but very neurotic. And her emotional life was all over the place. She told me a story that illustrates the healing power of love and close cooperation.

"I've been terrible since I was seventeen. I've only had one completely happy time in my life," she explained.

"When was it?" I asked.

"When I lived in the Gothic Quarter with an English boyfriend I had. He was a great guy but more neurotic than me. Most of the time, he was down. But I loved him and took care of him. And focusing on him, I forgot about myself, and I was happy."

THE EXAMPLE OF ALCOHOLICS ANONYMOUS

As a young psychologist, I studied addiction in depth. I explored many forms of therapy and fell in love with Alcoholics Anonymous. These groups, first created in the 1930s, use a method based on mutual cooperation.

They hold weekly – or even daily – meetings where members gain the strength and inspiration needed to stop drinking. Once sober, some become sponsors for a new member and commit to being available to them twenty-four hours a day, going to them wherever they are and at any time to remove them from temptation.

There are Alcoholics Anonymous groups all over the world, working miracles every day. I've met many doctors who have been amazed by how alcoholics have recovered from thirty years of daily intoxication that destroyed them inside and out. After following the Alcoholics Anonymous method for a time, they emerge transformed into new people, mentally balanced and strong, even physically improved.

I mention Alcoholics Anonymous groups in this chapter on depression and anxiety because they offer an incredible lesson on the power of virtue. Giving yourself to others is such a powerful force that it dilutes any physical or mental complaint, even the most savage withdrawal symptoms.

Because when we open ourselves up to virtue as a source of well-being, we gain independence from worldly pleasures. We no longer care if we're unable to enjoy a film, sex, or dinner with friends. Virtue becomes our favorite pleasure, shall we say.

People suffering from depression or anxiety say to themselves, "I'm done with this depression because I can't do anything!" or "This anxiety stops me from leading a normal life!" And that's what scares them, that being overwhelmed by these emotions limits them so much that their lives are a permanent punishment. But in the pursuit of virtue as a pleasure – and I'm talking about a higher pleasure than any other – this problem disappears. We can be very happy enjoying ourselves and our wonderful virtues, which give so much meaning to our lives!

Alcoholics Anonymous members describe a phenomenon that has always caught my attention. Through their work to give up alcohol, they reach what they call the "fourth dimension of existence," which equates to a level of well-being and happiness much higher than they ever imagined. Their new spiritual mindset allows them to discover a new way of life.

We can all adopt this orientation towards virtue, goodness, and beauty – more happiness and peace than we ever imagined.

ANXIETY IS NO DISADVANTAGE.

As we have seen, when we're suffering from anxiety or depression – or any symptom – we think this "emotional disaster" will prevent us from leading a normal life. If we're in a café and some cheerful, relaxed youngsters come in, full of energy, we look at them with envy and sadness: "I'm sick! Everyone else has their faculties and can enjoy life."

But this is not the rational way to approach the matter. Instead, we must say to ourselves, "My life's going to change. Through virtue, these symptoms are going to help me discover the fourth dimension of existence, which is a much better place."

In this chapter we learned that:

- Anxiety, depression, chronic fatigue and other complaints caused by the mind disappear when we stop being afraid of them.
- Whenever we think that a symptom has ruined our lives and that we can't be happy, we have to think, "My life's going to be better, just in a different way!"
- The pleasure of virtue is superior to any other. We can be very happy even with depression or anxiety when we orient ourselves towards virtue.
- Some of the virtues that help us lose our fear of depression or anxiety are loving our partner, total honesty and giving oneself to others.

15
A New Conflictology

A dervish and his disciple were walking along a quiet road. In the distance, they saw a cloud of dust: an elegant carriage drawn by four white horses was approaching at full speed. As it came closer, they realized that it wasn't slowing or moving away from the middle of the road. Within a minute, it was upon them, so they leaped into a ditch. When they got up, they saw the carriage move away, raising more dust, this time onto their clothes.

The disciple was about to curse them, but before he could, his master got in ahead of him and said, "May your lives fill you with happiness!"

The young man, surprised, asked, "Why do you wish happiness to those reprobates? They almost ran us over!"

"Do you really think they would go around bothering everyone if they were happy?" his master replied serenely.

Some time ago, I had a disagreement with one of my most beloved relatives. He was important to me because, although we're cousins, from a young age Francesc and I have been like brothers.

I will always remember our wonderful summers in Lleida: we learned to ride bikes together and had a secret cabin in the woods; as teenagers, we discovered nocturnal escapades and flings with girls.

Happiness Declassified

What happened was that my grandparents handed down an apartment to their grandchildren. It was their main residence, which, for bureaucratic reasons, they had put in Francesc's name. When they died, we all wanted to sell it, except for Francesc, who objected. And he had the power to do so. Although the will said that our grandparents were leaving the property to all of us, legally, the apartment didn't belong to us because it was in my cousin's name.

Blinded by greed and using cheap excuses, Francesc decided that the property was his. Even his parents – my aunt and uncle – were embarrassed by his behavior. All the grandchildren reacted with anger and indignation to our cousin's legal "theft," but he seemed more than willing to fall out over it. At one point, he even said, "Everyone here is looking out for themselves, so I'm going to do the same. My real family are my wife and son, no one else." At the time, there was talk of taking Francesc to court and no longer speaking to him. How could we continue to have a relationship with such a selfish person, capable of stealing from his loved ones?

At first, I joined the call to war. I even put forward the name of a lawyer I knew. But thanks to a stroke of good sense, I was able to change to a completely different perspective. The cognitive principles of *unconditional acceptance of others* and *the power of letting go* helped me see a non-violent solution that, in addition to giving us a better chance of success, would make us all stronger.

We would all write a monthly letter to Francesc saying more or less the following:

Dear Francesc,

You are a wonderful person. You are full of beauty inside. I love you.

I'm writing to you today about the issue of our grandparents' inheritance. Wouldn't it be better to share it among all their grandchildren as they wished? We all do crazy things sometimes and a dark part of our mind tells us to commit an injustice. I know because I'm the first person it can happen to. I confess to you that I once stole. But sooner or later, we discover that radical honesty makes us happier and gives better results.

But now comes the most important part of this letter: believe me, Francesc, if you can't see this matter as I do, I swear I'll love you just the same because your love is much more important than money. I will always be by your side. More so, in fact.

How my brothers and cousins reacted when I showed them the letter! They thought I was on drugs or had joined the Hare Krishna. Or both at the same time.

But the interesting thing is what happened next. I was the first to send the rational missive, and a month later, my uncle, Francesc's father, called me.

"Hello, Rafael. You'll never guess what happened! A couple of days ago, Francesc told me to meet him at the notary's office. He didn't want to tell me why. When I arrived, everything was ready: your grandparents' apartment is now in my name. He has asked me to sell it for the best possible price and share the money with the grandchildren. But the craziest thing is, he's giving it all up. He doesn't want his share."

"Seriously?" I said, surprised. But we can't allow that. We have to give him his part."

"Of course, we'll do that. I'll drag him kicking and screaming to the bank if I have to. Francesc is a good kid, you know him, but he loses his bearings sometimes. You know? After the notary, we went for a beer, and he showed me the letter you sent him. He told me how much he loved you, and the idiot started crying. Incredible, don't you think?"

With the love letter ploy, within a few weeks, Francesc came to his senses, and we all learned a great lesson in conflict resolution.

NEW AND OLD CONFLICT RESOLUTION

There are hundreds, perhaps thousands, of manuals on conflict resolution. Studies on reconciliation between people, organizations, or nations.

I read some, but they didn't offer much to me. The vast majority are based on a mistaken or, at least, dysfunctional worldview. They have good intentions, but they focus on what they call a *win-win* approach. *I win, you win,* sounds good, and it's certainly better than *I win, you lose*, but the approach I'm going to propose here is distinctly superior: much better for our mental health and much more effective. It's the *no-win-love* approach.

This new approach – which is actually as old as the religions – requires us to give up material gains in favour of love and reap the rewards in the medium and long term. I can assure you that it works in about 80% of cases, and it also improves mental health.

The win-win approach proposes that, faced with a conflict of interests, we should step back and propose solutions in which both parties gain. In the case of the issue with our inheritance, the aim would have been to put more on the table so that my cousin conceded but also felt like he was winning. For example, proposing to sell the apartment and investing the money in a joint fund to earn more in the long term.

Win-win solutions aren't bad because they're more or less reconciliatory, and their aim is not revenge or justice. But they still have a problem: they feed our personal weakness by attaching too much importance to material gain. Remember, necessititis makes us weak, and letting go makes us strong.

And once again, I can assure you that the no-win-love method is, paradoxically, more beneficial than win-win. We must move on from the avenging method that's predominant in our society. This approach, which consists of forcefully demanding one's rights, is only 20% effective, and it makes us all neurotic and aggressive.

DEMANDING IS PROHIBITED

The *no-win-love* method is the *suggestion* model, as opposed to the *demand* model, and it consists of:

- Never catastrophizing. Never tell ourselves that we cannot bear others doing dishonest things. Of course, we can! We need very little to be happy – we certainly don't need everyone to treat us well all of the time!

- Practicing *unconditional acceptance of others*. In other words, loving everyone with their flaws because we're all imperfect and, at the same time, amazing.

- Never triggering one another's demands in a spiral of constant super-demands. When demands are made of us, we instinctively want to make a counter-demand: "You're demanding I be fair in this, and I will do so only when you're fair in that." But when we receive a suggestion with love, we open ourselves up to change.

- Using good teaching skills and the enjoyable art of persuasion.

- Resolving conflicts with no emotional cost and without using force. It's better to enjoy the process, learn and grow.

Let's take a look at the traditional style of conflict resolution, which is not the *win-win* approach described above but the justice approach or the John Wayne method. It essentially consists of demanding that the other party behave decently. That they change their attitude, or we will force them to do so. And if we can't force them, rest assured, we'll get our revenge. And, finally, if our revenge doesn't leave us satisfied, we'll break relations. The engine of the justice approach is our "I can't bear it"; the fuel is the deification of the concept of justice, and the lubricant is our fear of letting go.

The suggestion approach (no win-love) or *Dalai Lama method*, on the other hand, consists of trying to persuade with love, activating our ability to let go beforehand. This approach is mentally empowering because it means that we do not need the other party to change in order to be happy; we do not need to be treated well or fairly. If they concede, we gain a fairer friend; if they don't, we love them just the same. There's no anger or disappointment.

At first, my cousins and siblings didn't understand the suggestion method and they asked, "But if Francesc ignores the letters and keeps the apartment to himself, what are we going to do?"

"Love him anyway because we don't need him to be any other way," I replied.

"And that's it? He'll love that! It's like telling him he's right!" yelled my brother Gonzalo, red with rage.

"No, not at all! We won't say he's right because until he changes his mind, we'll keep sending him the letters indefinitely," I pointed out.

"But if we keep insisting on the little notes, he might stop talking to us," said Belén, Francesc's sister, worried that the relationship would be ruined even more.

"That's his business, but we'll love him all the same. If he turns his back on us because of our loving guidance, it will be a shame, but we will always open our hearts to him," I concluded.

THE DALAI LAMA METHOD

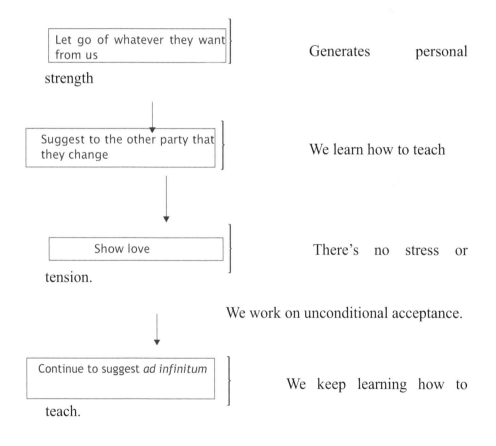

Let go of whatever they want from us	Generates personal strength
Suggest to the other party that they change	We learn how to teach
Show love	There's no stress or tension.
	We work on unconditional acceptance.
Continue to suggest *ad infinitum*	We keep learning how to teach.

GANDHI AND NON-VIOLENCE

Some years ago, I discovered Mahatma Gandhi's thinking. I read his autobiography and was fascinated by this little man who, despite being a renowned lawyer, wore a loincloth and a white sheet, the clothes of India's poor.

Gandhi called his philosophy "non-violence," and what he proposed, very briefly, was to respond to injustice with kindness, to mistreatment, with warmth. And at the same time, to go to great lengths to educate the other party about the superiority of cooperation over selfishness. With this strategy, Gandhi achieved something amazing: India's independence from a violent United Kingdom without firing a single shot. But the most important point was that he managed to find his own peace and reach a higher level of fulfillment.

According to Gandhi, non-violence begins with understanding that people behave dishonestly only out of confusion or madness. When we're selfish, we're like a four-year-old child behaving self-centredly. We have to grow up.

I remember once asking a patient who had a conflict with her sister, "What would you say to a child who doesn't want to share their cake with their party guests?"

"That's easy. That if you hide in the corner and eat all the cake, you won't enjoy it as much as if you share it with your friends. And if you share now, your friends will invite you to their parties later, with more cakes and more fun," she said, laughing.

"Well, your sister is behaving like a four-year-old girl who still doesn't know the advantages of cooperation. But we can show her. If she grasps it, I'm sure she'll change," I added.

WE'RE ALL LITTLE DEVILS.

A scorpion was standing at a river's edge. He was eager to cross it, for he was on his way to the annual scorpion dance. A ray of hope lit up his mind when he saw a frog floating on the water on a large oak leaf.

"Friend," he said, "can you help me cross? If you carry me on your back, it will only take a couple of jumps."

"What?! I haven't gone crazy yet! You're a scorpion. If I let you on my back, you'll prick me with your deadly sting."

"Of course I won't! How could you think that? If I did, you'd die, and we'd both sink."

After some thought, the frog agreed. The scorpion seemed like a nice guy. So she let him perch on her slippery back, and they began to cross the river.

Halfway across, in a turbulent spot, the scorpion turned red, raised his sting, and drove it deep into the frog.

The frog felt the poison penetrate her veins, and her strength left her. She only had one breath, and she wanted to ask, "Why did you do it? We're both going under!"

The scorpion, panicking at his imminent death, replied, "Dammit! Because it's my nature!"

The philosophy of non-violence involves recognizing that we all make mistakes because that is our nature! In fact, if we were perfect, life would have no charm; it would be strange and boring.

Indeed, our lives are peppered with mistakes: selfishness, outbursts, jealousy, absurd aggression. Even when we always try to be kind, we sometimes interfere where we're not wanted. As the great Oscar Wilde said, "It is always with the best intentions that the worst work is done."

But none of those things are essential to anyone's happiness. In reality, they're trivial. In the process of improving ourselves, we discover new, more authentic, beautiful, and exciting ways to live. Mistakes are a wonderful opportunity to keep growing.

When we become demanding, we hold the absurd belief that others' flaws are intolerable while ours are minor. We're very lenient towards ourselves and unforgiving of others. We often say to ourselves, "I would never do that!" to highlight the severity of the other person's sin. And we don't realise that we're being unfair: it's normal for everyone to have different flaws; it would be strange if we didn't.

It's true Francesc was capable of ripping off his entire family, and that's something I would never do, but an honest examination of myself tells me that I'm capable of other dishonest actions: different, but also unacceptable. And neither he nor I are bad people; we're just four-year-olds who still have a lot to learn. Perhaps together, with loving guidance, we can go far in our journey towards generosity.

This is the principle of Unconditional Other Acceptance (UOA): we're all good by nature, and when we're not, it's out of madness or ignorance. We're childish, or we've lost our minds. Or both.

UOA is very important in cognitive psychology because it is only by accepting others that we can have unconditional acceptance of ourselves, or in other words, treat ourselves kindly when we fail. Not beating ourselves up stupidly when we make mistakes is essential for strong self-esteem. And we will only be kind to ourselves and guide ourselves well when we do the same with others. People who punish others also punish themselves, and vice versa.

In fact, I persuaded my family to use the suggestion approach on the grounds that the strategy would make us strong and happy, first and foremost.

"Treating Francesc with affection, whatever happens, will make us treat ourselves with affection when we fail," I said in a family meeting.

"But what if he never changes?" they asked.

"Bad luck, but we will have done something important for ourselves."

THE BAD GUYS' PRIEST

Some time ago, I watched an episode of the Spanish TV show *Salvados* that gave an incredible example of UOA. The programme was entitled *Qué pasa después de la cárcel? ("What happens after prison?"*, it's available on YouTube*)* and the part that fascinated me was an interview with the priest Josep Maria Fabró. I take my hat off to him.

The premise of the show was that the penitentiary system does not work because it's designed to punish and not rehabilitate, as the extremely high rates of reoffending show. A number of arguments were put forward to demonstrate it.

But then the presenter Jordi Évole interviewed Josep Maria Fabró and things took a much more profound turn. Because this priest is one of the few people (in the world, perhaps) who understands the importance of the concept of UOA. Jordi Évole went to Josep Maria's house in Martorell, an industrial town on the outskirts of Barcelona. The conversation they had, summarising, was as follows:

JORDI ÉVOLE: What is this house we're in?

JOSEP MARIA: It's a shelter for people who have served a prison sentence and have nowhere to go.

J. É: And how long do they spend here?

J. M: It's a temporary thing – five or six months – although sometimes it's much longer. But in theory, this refuge is to help people reintegrate into society, find a job

J. É: And how do you choose who can come to live with you? Because it only has six places.

J. M: I don't choose them! The social workers at the prison called me and said, "Josep Maria, we have this person who has nowhere to go, and it will be very difficult to find a place for him." And we take in whoever it is, whoever they ask us to take!

J. É: And why is it not a problem to take in whoever they ask you to?

J. M: Because if it was a problem, the entire purpose of this house would fall apart. We can't say, "I don't want that one, or that one, because he's too bad."

J. É: But that must have brought you problems...

J. M: Of course! I've seen it all here. People who got drunk and smashed the house up. Once, a man overdosed. Anyway

J. É: Father, would you take in the notorious murderer and rapist they call *El Loco del Chandal*, the Tracksuit Madman?

J. M: Yes! Of course. In fact, I've known him since he was a kid and started going to prison. He's from around here.

J. É: But people like him, society rejects them.

J. M: Yes, I know. There was a demonstration against him recently where they yelled, "Son of a bitch! Murderer! Rapist!" But what's the point of all of that?

J. É: Martorell residents complain that El Loco del Chandal hasn't been rehabilitated and he's a danger.

J. M: It's true that he refused any therapy and is certainly a danger. But now that he has served his sentence, should we give him a hand or not? Do we need to help him, or do we refuse? If we do that, we're condemning him a second time. I see these people's faces, and all I know is that they need to be given a hand however we can. And giving them a hand has its risks, of course.

J. É: Father, imagine you are with a victim of one of these criminals, and they say, "It seems wrong to me that you were helping him when he harmed me so much. He's a bad person." What would you say?

J. M: Well, if he is a bad person, that is all the more reason to continue to want to help him and be by his side.

Happiness Declassified

J. É: Does everyone deserve a second chance, even if they haven't been rehabilitated and have committed the most horrific crime?

J. M: Of course they do. Another opportunity. And if necessary, one more. And another. And every time they fall, we will help them get up again as many times as they need.

Every time I watch this interview, I'm moved because it exemplifies true love for the most persecuted people in the world, those we detest, who we consider "non-human." They're the lowest class of people, far worse than the untouchables of India. And all this hatred and rejection, to a large extent, comes from fear.

And fear is always an enemy of happiness! If we lose our fear of losing what we have, in this case, our own physical integrity, there's no obstacle to loving everyone and understanding that aggressors are simply sick and those most in need of help.

Our fear of being attacked, of being killed, is quite irrational because it will inevitably happen anyway. Life itself will take care of it. We'll all get sick and die, and that's okay. The important thing is to be happy in spite of it. We don't see that trying to strangle the snake is the same as trying to asphyxiate ourselves because we all have the seed of love but also the seed of sickness. But let's be reassured, the most beautiful flowers grow on the moors. Josep Maria Fabró is one of them. For strong and happy people, the risks associated with giving a helping hand to madmen are insignificant. Because, in reality, no one can harm us in our most essential place: our inner fortress.

LETTING GO

In almost all my books I have written this sentence: "Strength is in letting go." And with every day that passes, I believe in it more. Perhaps the fundamental principle of cognitive therapy is this: *We need very little to be happy.* Almost all our visualization exercises serve this purpose: we imagine ourselves being happy in a wheelchair, in a cheap hostel.

If we're able to enjoy life with very little, nothing can scare us. It's why the philosopher Diogenes lived in a barrel – to show himself that happiness is in the mind, not in comfort or status, not even in physical integrity.

When we joyfully let go of an asset, dozens of windows are opened. Life is incredibly abundant when we stop clinging to just one kind of enjoyment. Letting go means accepting what life takes away from you but making the most of what it gives you. In relation to others, we can let go of the idea that they must treat us well but remain serene and cheerful, expecting immediate and greater rewards in the form of maturity and fulfillment.

After letting go, the next step in the suggestion method, to "suggest a change in the other party," teaches us how to be teachers and how to influence others.

BEING A DIFFERENT KIND OF BOSS

For some time, I have been giving talks to companies that want to introduce rational concepts to their staff. And one of the key points when it comes to changing an entire organization is the leadership style.

I call good bosses *modeling bosses* because they base their strategy on *modeling* for their employees, not on *being in charge*. And they model with joy, persuasive skills, and enthusiasm. The same educational strategy that a good parent or teacher adopts with their children. A modeling leader builds on the following premises:

- Everyone enjoys doing things well, excelling at something
- We all want to be involved in an exciting project

Rational bosses offer their employees these two opportunities: to be part of an excellent work dynamic and to be involved in something beautiful because there's nothing better than having a job in which you can be fulfilled with authenticity. Always positive always confident in their abilities, modelling bosses lead them towards these two destinations. They show them how they can work in an extraordinary way. No one can resist the temptation to be excellent!

I once employed an assistant to take care of my office work: accounting, admin for my psychology practice, press relations, etc. His name was Arturo, and he was a young journalism graduate who I liked a lot. He was the first person I had employed in my life, and I wasn't sure how to handle it.

At first, Arturo made mistakes that annoyed me: he worked from home, and when I called him, I could never reach him; he left important business to the last minute and generally gave the impression that he wasn't making much effort. But to be a modeling boss, I resisted my initial impulse to fire him – a rash impulse – and did the following:

- Design the model
- Sell the idea
- Redesign it

THE BEST EMPLOYEE IN SPAIN

The first step was to spend a few hours designing what the perfect assistant would look like for me, and I wrote a description accordingly:

Dear Arturo,

I've designed the following profile for your position. I think we have the opportunity to work according to this model, which is the bee's knees: we're going to make our office the best-run in Spain. Like the offices of the great leaders, can you imagine? Like Obama's! It would be great if all our procedures flowed in an easy and orderly way so that we could do a great job at every level.

How about dividing the various tasks into departments and designing better processes each week? Accounting, for example, is well-organized and clear.

Checking each step and having a very fluid relationship with our financial advisor, who will give you all the information you need (you can call him every day to ask him for details).

It would also be great to improve our organization, having everything in clearly marked folders. One of these days, I'll give you some training on David Allen's book Getting Things Done, and you'll see how fantastic it is to keep your diary up to date.

You can self-manage your work so that you have a great time and learn continuously. What do you think about working really hard for the six hours of your morning shift?

Wouldn't that be great? We have the opportunity to create a modern psychology practice that is well above the standard in Spain, with happy and excellent staff who are always learning and highly motivated. You will be a key player in these improvements! I'm sure of it!

On the subject of our communication, it would be great if you were always available. That way, if something unexpected or urgent comes up, I'll feel confident and at ease. This is very valuable to me. You can do this by always carrying your mobile phone with you or by focusing exclusively on your work in the mornings. In the afternoon, you can keep your phone close by to quickly respond to any specific issues. Do you think that's a good idea? Is that possible?

It would also be great if we could improve timeliness. In other words, take steps long in advance. For example, we could buy airline tickets two weeks ahead. That would give me a fantastic sense of efficiency and peace of mind.

As for your working hours, it would be excellent if you could complete the six hours every day, without skipping any. You would get an extraordinary amount done this way and become an incredible and exemplary assistant, the best, perhaps. I think it would be very good if you kept strictly to your schedule because two of the keys to success are perseverance and consistency. What do you think? When we start to flag, we lose that excellence. The key is to say "no" to any distractions during office hours.

Excellence is not hard to achieve – we just have to put passion, enthusiasm, and strength into it. I have a very clear vision of our work together.

I decided to send Arturo these job descriptions every fortnight. Each time, the suggestions were different, but with the same vision of excellence and enjoyment, and with the ideas and instruction I thought appropriate.

It's very important that we convince employees – or our children – of the advantages of working in an excellent way, especially for themselves. Motivate them: show them that they can achieve wonderful levels of enjoyment and excellence. We must show them how to do their tasks wholeheartedly and paint them the idyllic scene of pride in a job well done, commitment, and authenticity. Always aiming high.

In short, the first step in modeling leadership is to sell the idea, appealing to the desire to do excellent work. The second, "designing the model," is about showing them how to do it. The third step is to insist on these two points periodically until they reach the standard we want. Being a boss is about mobilizing forces, molding people like clay statues, and persevering with joy and optimism.

THE GURU-BOSS

I once met an extraordinary boss. He was the director of a publishing house. I did an internship in the company when I was young, just after finishing my psychology studies. The boss, whose name was Jordi, spoke to employees about his vision for the publishing house, his commitment to making meaningful books, and personal stories about his work. He would spend at least half an hour a day doing this. The result was that Jordi's team was super motivated, to the point that their work gave meaning to their lives; they felt alive, part of an exciting project. I've never seen anything like it since.

Jordi's staff would arrive an hour before their shift and stay until 9 or 10 p.m.

I had a great time when I was there and felt like I was on an adventure, a trip abroad, or something like that.

This is how powerful the effect of an inspiring boss can be. The basic principles of their influence are:

- Never reprimand anyone, tell them off, or make faces at them.
- Always be positive: point out the employee's fabulous potential.
- Teach employees that work can be a unique adventure.
- Be an educator: show the way again and again.

One of the problems that companies have – and that we have in personal relationships in general – is that we often follow criteria such as, "I must choose employees/friends/family who are worthy," instead of, "I'm going to help these people become incredible employees'/friends'/ family."

The difference is crucial because, with a defenestration approach – in the purest Soviet style –bosses focus on the negatives and not the positives. In doing so, they develop not their teaching skills but merely their ability to slit employees' throats. Rational bosses, on the other hand, focus on the positives and are true educators.

Soviet bosses – who send anyone who makes a mistake to Siberia – are paranoid because they're too error-focused. They concentrate too much on failure and want people to be competent as soon as they arrive. These guys have a terrible time – they're almost always angry and stressed. And it puts others on edge. Rational bosses have the mental space to enjoy themselves at work, and it's a pleasure for them to teach their employees: they model for them until they become aces, leading to fabulous overall results.

Let's put an end to the gulags. Hurrah for fun!

RATIONAL SCHOOLS

I was once invited to lead a workshop at a posh school in Madrid. Sitting in the psychology coordinator's office, I was informed of the difficult cases. They told me about Feliciano, an arrogant sixteen-year-old who enjoyed breaking the rules. As they explained to me, the boy felt immune: he was the son of a powerful person and had influence over the school management.

The coordinator told me, "His tutor's nerves are frayed. She's in a constant arm wrestle with him but never manages to assert herself."

"Tell me about a recent conflict," I requested.

"Recently, the whole class went skiing. One day, Feliciano and his little group arrived two hours late to catch the bus that would take them to the piste. The rest of the class had to wait for them at the hotel, and they were very angry. The teacher told him off and he ignored her as ever. There was a big row, but Feliciano couldn't care less about anything. What can we say to the teacher?" she asked me.

"Well, she has to learn to be a modeling leader, not a neurotic one, as she is now. Feliciano, like the others, should not be reprimanded for his failures or have them exaggerated but guided towards the ideal that he can become," I said.

"But how can we not reprimand him? All the kids were annoyed that they couldn't go skiing," she pointed out.

"And is that so bad? The rest need to be taught that we can happily let go. I would have sat them on the floor to give them an impromptu emotional education class. I would have explained that we don't need to go skiing and that Feliciano is confused or going through a childish patch. Our common project would be to help Feliciano out of his confusion. At the very least, attempting it would be very interesting for everyone," I explained.

"And what would you have said to Feliciano?" the teacher asked me.

"When he arrived, I would have ended the emotional education lesson and said to him, 'Dear student, I would like you to be more attentive to the group and behave in a considerate way with everyone; I can teach you to do it, and it will be very useful for you in life, but if you don't do it, I'll appreciate you all the same. Anyway! Let's go skiing, guys; it's time to have some fun!" I added.

The school psychologists in the room looked at me with open mouths. I don't think they had ever heard of such an approach. Then the coordinator said, "Ugh! That's all very well, Rafael, but I think it will be hard to persuade this teacher to use this modeling strategy. She's very set on her disciplinary method."

"Yes, and how has that gone? Has this kid changed over the course of the year?" I asked.

"No, not at all. On the contrary, he's increasingly rebellious," she replied.

"She's behaving in a childish way, too, as if she has to impose her authority on her student. No one needs to impose anything! The aim is to model a virtuous, successful, happy person and guide him there enthusiastically. Suppose it doesn't work; bad luck. But I'm certain that she'll have more success this way than she has had so far," I concluded.

Because changing a person through force is a mediocre approach that will only produce mediocre results, no one becomes a fantastic musician out of obligation! To become excellent at something, it has to be a voluntary decision driven by excitement. Rational leaders are people who offer this vision to others. They open their eyes to a higher, happier way of working. Feliciano needed to be treated like a rough diamond, which is what he is, with the potential to be a wonderful student. Perseverance is the mother of success. So, every time he was rude and arrogant, he needed to be encouraged to change, showing that cooperation was a better way, but with joy and love. No arm wrestles or impositions!

And it's important to avoid becoming agitated. The teacher was becoming hypersensitive to the small discomforts of her work and was annoyed by something that could be precisely the most interesting part of the job: teaching students to transform themselves to become excellent people.

In this chapter we learned that:

- The *no win-love* method is the best way to resolve conflicts and consists of:

a) Never catastrophising. Never telling ourselves that we can't bear others doing dishonest things.

b) Practising unconditional acceptance of others. In other words, loving everyone with their defects.

c) Never triggering the other party's demands in a spiral of constant super-demands.

d) Being a good teacher, using the power of persuasion.

e) Resolving conflicts at no emotional cost. Instead, enjoying the process, learning and growing.

- The best way to behave as a boss is to educate and motivate every employee to become an ace.

- Faced with poor performance, good bosses are unruffled. They ask themselves, "How can I train my workers better so this doesn't happen again?"

- Faced with a wayward student, good teachers are unruffled. They ask themselves, "How can I be more persuasive so the kids become more mature?"

16
Learning to Negotiate

One day, Mullah Nasreddin visited hell and was astounded by what he saw there. There were a lot of people sitting around a lavish table. It was covered in dishes, each more exquisite than the other. But they all looked emaciated.

They were starving! The problem was they had to eat with chopsticks as long as oars, and when they picked up the food, they were unable to put it in their mouths.

After this, Nasreddin ascended to heaven. To his great astonishment, there was another table there covered in delicacies that the people also ate with chopsticks as long as oars. Now, however, everyone looked healthy. Here, when they picked up the food, they fed it to the people next to them.

In this chapter, we're going to broach a subject that, though it may seem so, is far from trivial. We're going to learn to negotiate and share ideas, which is an essential skill for good mental health for two reasons: First, because generally, we don't know how to do it, and we often cause arguments that ruin moments that could be beautiful. And second – and more importantly – because we're going to change the way we understand human relationships: we're going to learn to enjoy people and handle difficult people with skill. It's worth doing!

I remember the case of two friends of mine from my youth, Anna and Juanma. Two fabulous people, classmates from psychology school, who started going out with each other when we were twenty years old. Anna and Juanma loved each other, and they understood each other very well, but from the outset, their relationship was an infernal chaos. The problem was that they argued furiously all the time. Almost all their interactions were like this:

"Juanma, slow down! You know I don't like it when you drive like this!"

"Are you kidding me? I'm driving normally!" he replied, offended and resentful. "And don't yell at me, especially not in the car!"

"You're driving too fast! Stop right now – I'm getting out! And I wasn't yelling at you; you're paranoid, man!"

"If you get out here, don't bother calling me again, Madam Angry! I'm sick of you ordering me around!" he yelled, losing his temper.

Separately, Anna and Juanma were soft and kind, but together, they were always making a spectacle. They fought in the lecture halls, in the cafeteria, at a concert, on the beach, and at the theatre; I think the only place they didn't row was in bed, where they usually ended up resolving their disagreements. In less than a year, they realized they were better apart than together.

Throughout my professional career, I've seen many cases like this. Couples who don't know how to resolve their differences, an essential skill in any union. And this lack of negotiation skills doesn't just affect couples, but every other kind of human relationship. Just think of family gatherings, where political debates often turn into absurd arguments.

Most people don't know how to have a discussion; they don't know how to share ideas. And that makes us inflexible, stubborn, arrogant, unhappy, and very bad at resolving conflicts. In this chapter we will learn to do it differently, with a style that will change our interactions forever, as well as our minds as a whole, which will become more flexible and creative.

INCLUSIVE DIALOGUE

I call the basic technique for debating effectively *inclusive dialogue*. It's how the smartest people debate! It essentially consists of always trying to see the other person's truth before putting forward our own. It involves listening to the other person FIRST before wanting to be right. When we focus first on them and their truth, we become truly influential people!

Let's look at an example. My father is a lovely man. He offers everyone the warmth typical of a mountain person. He is genuinely interested in others and their lives. But, like many people of his generation, he has a flaw: he still thinks that "Life was better under Franco!" I have lost count of the number of arguments his fascist fixation has caused because there was a time when, at every family lunch, we fell out over the same old subject. At some point, my father would start defending the dictatorship, and, of course, his five children took the bait, and the discussion became absurdly heated until we learned to use the "inclusive dialogue" technique.

Inclusive dialogue consists of thinking – before saying anything – about the point the person we disagree with may have. For instance, what truth is there in saying "life was better under Franco"? Finding out is what an emotionally intelligent person would do.

No one is right!

"Truth" is a slippery thing. There is not one truth, but many, even for scientific phenomena. Indeed, scientific explanations are under constant review. Other truths, the ones you hear on the street, are even more imperfect. What we think – about politics, ethics, relationships, and so on – depends on our viewpoint and generation. They tend to be outlooks that, within a few decades, become outdated. Intelligent people know this and take it into account. Rash, stubborn people, don't.

No one is completely right about anything, ever!

What we can do is reach agreements and draw useful conclusions that give us a good outlook on reality. That's all. There are no absolute truths, no "I'm right," no "I'm clever, you're stupid"!

In this sense, even my father is right to think life was better under Franco. And I learned to accept it before offering him a new perspective. Whenever the subject came up, I would say, "Dad, it's true that public safety was good at that time." And it wasn't a trick to win over my father. I really believe it and I would convey this to him.

Then I would go on, "And you're right that the later years saw an economic boom. The splendid 1970s!"

To get to grips with another person's truth, we have to try to understand why they think that way, what experiences have given them their ideas, and finally, recognize what may actually be in it. There's always some truth in what other people say because they experienced the evidence! And reality has many nooks and crannies.

Only after recognizing the other person's truth may we lay ours on the table.

"But you must admit, *Papá*, that with your five children, you've seen a very nice part of democracy. Four of your children went to university for the first time in the family's history. And I even studied at two foreign universities. In Franco's time, that was very difficult. His system preferred class separation: the rich had a monopoly on good education."

"That's true, son. Yes, it didn't suit the ruling class for the poor to study with the elite! And that was very wrong," he admitted.

At last! My father was open to considering a reality other than his own when it came to politics. But it was only possible the day I made a real effort to understand his truth.

A TECHNIQUE IN THREE STEPS

The inclusive dialogue technique has three stages:

- Search for the other person's truth
- Offer our view
- Include the other person in our world

The first step is the most difficult because it is where genuine mental openness takes place, where we learn to be more intelligent and mentally healthy people. Finding the other person's truth is also an exercise in humility that we're unused to. We've been taught to want to "be right" to "argue our point," which is stupid because no one is completely right.

On one occasion, I was giving a lecture, and when it was time for questions, the issue of abortion came up. I'm in favor of a gestational limit, or in other words, that abortion should be legal up to three months of gestation, or twenty-two weeks, in the exceptional cases set out in Spanish law: serious malformation and a risk to the pregnant woman's health. But in the audience, there was a woman in her fifties named Pilar who objected to my view.

"Abortion is always murder! We should never kill a child just because it poses a risk to the mother or because it's not perfect! No one is!" she said, visibly angry.

While the woman spoke, I considered her position. Why, with all her goodwill, was she flatly opposed to any kind of abortion? I looked at her and saw that she was a beautiful and elegant woman. No doubt she was a fantastic mother!

I didn't have long to get into her mind and put myself in her place, but when you leave aside the absurd need to be right, it's not hard. "What truth is there in the anti-abortionist stance?" I asked myself. I quickly grasped it and said, "You know what, Pilar? I love that there are people in the world as generous as you, willing to stand up for children and the unborn. And I understand your position. It's true that life must often be protected from its creators – the parents themselves. It wouldn't be nice if we didn't worry about the little ones." And then I expressed another reality that I also believe is important in this issue. "But, Pilar, how about this? I've read in many anthropology books that Amazonian people, who live in groups of around a hundred individuals in total harmony with nature, perform infanticides at the moment of birth. And they do it when there's a danger the tribe will grow more than it should."

"I think that's a horrific murder!" the woman blurted out.

"Of course, from our point of view, it is. But anthropologists explain that, for the Amazonian Indians, controlling the size of the tribe is essential because the survival of the group depends on it," I added as gently as I could. "What would you do if this were true and, to save one, everyone had to die?"

"I wouldn't kill the child. Let God's will be done!" she replied, still upset.

"Your position is beautiful, Pilar! And for the record, I am also in favour of life and unconditional love. But I was just telling you about this practice so we can see that every situation deserves a different reading, don't you think?"

"But we don't live in the Amazon like a tribe now! We have a lot of resources to help families with problems," she argued.

"You're absolutely right! I just wanted to illustrate that, in moral or ethical matters, there are often two interests that can clash: the good of the community and the good of the individual. Sometimes, the paradox occurs that, in seeking the good of the individual, we cause trouble for everyone else. That can happen, can't it, Pilar?"

"But I'll say again that we can respect all lives nowadays because we have the means to do so," she said, her temper still frayed.

"You know what, Pilar? I'd love to have a beer with you someday. You're fantastic!" I said to finish the conversation and be able to continue with the round of questions.

Then she laughed a little and said, "I accept your invitation! But I won't change my mind."

"There's no need to! I love that there are people as generous as you! And if you like, we can agree that children often need to be protected from their own parents! And that's a responsibility of the group," I concluded.

After the lecture, we chatted for a while, and I got to know her a bit more. As I imagined, she was an exceptional person. And I saw that she was already much closer to my position.

"Well, the issue of abortion is complex; you're right," she said. "I'll think about it some more. Can you recommend some of the anthropology books that you mentioned?"

Inclusive dialogue requires us to delve into the other person's ideology to extract the truth in it and, after connecting on this level, offer what we have found ourselves. The aim is to lead the other person to another broader truth that includes their own. This is why we call it *inclusive dialogue* – because we include their truth within our own, making it broader, with more perspective.

Inclusive dialogue goes something like this:

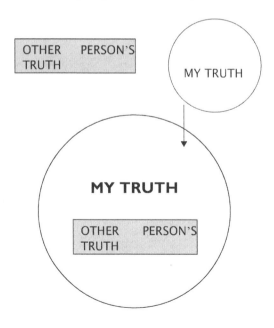

Including the other person in our world means telling them in some way that, despite our differences, we love them just the same. Within cognitive psychology, this is related to our concept of *unconditional acceptance*. In my discussion about abortion, my inclusive maneuver was to express my desire to have a beer with her.

Inclusion in our world is a very important part of inclusive dialogue because, when we argue in an obstinate way, we almost always push the other person away. It's like saying, "You can't be my friend anymore because we're too different!" Sometimes, we do it with body language and tone of voice.

To avoid this distancing effect, it's very important to express the opposite. Couples who have good communication make the effort to say affectionate things when a disagreement arises. Something like, "Honey, I still think it's preferable to do this or that." And if we accompany the "honey" with a loving gesture, all the better.

Another way to express that we're including the other person even though we don't agree with them is by calling them by their first name. For example, with the lady I discussed abortion with, I tried to call her by her name every time I spoke. It's an expression of familiarity that shows our inclusive disposition.

Inclusive dialogue is the smartest and healthiest way to debate. To master it, we will have to practice a lot, but we can start right now with our families, friends, or work colleagues.

THE INCLUSIVE DIALOGUE MODEL

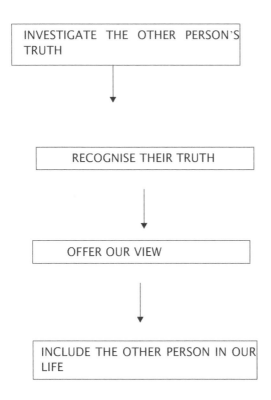

INVESTIGATE THE OTHER PERSON'S TRUTH

RECOGNISE THEIR TRUTH

OFFER OUR VIEW

INCLUDE THE OTHER PERSON IN OUR LIFE

A MEMBER OF THE PSOE AND THE PP

Our society neurotically promotes exclusionary dialogue. Just watch the television debates. The models they offer are typical of the most ignorant narrow-mindedness: believing oneself to be in possession of truths that nullify the other person's. It's like they're saying, "What an idiot you are!" and "Look how clever I am!" And that's a mistake because no one is clever in everything all of the time. And we're all stupid or ignorant at some time or another.

Psychologist and priest Anthony de Mello said that he was going to write a book entitled *I'm an Ass, You're an Ass!* He wanted to express exactly that: nothing is black and white; we're all smart and ignorant. It's much more intelligent to recognize it.

The more I build cognitive psychology into my life, the more it seems to me that politics would be much better if we stopped excluding others. In this sense, I consider myself sympathetic to all the political parties that exist in Spain. I could be a member of any of them: PP, PSOE,[1] Podemos, Izquierda Unida, Convergència, PNV... all of them! Because I'm on the right but also on the left. I believe in a unified Spanish state but also in Catalan and Basque independence, but I'm also the total opposite: a Spanish, Catalan, and Basque anti-nationalist.

All of these stances are partly right. It's true that solidarity is wonderful, but we can also get too used to scrounging. If we take everyone's realities into account, we can build explanation models that are increasingly broad and more likely to achieve a resolution. We are very close to a better model, like Einstein's theory of general relativity, which resolved the incompatibility between Newtonian mechanics and electromagnetism. It was a higher level of explanation because it accounted for more than the other two separately.

PSOE (Spanish Socialist Workers' Party) and PP (People's Party) are the two main and most dominant political parties in Spain, comparable to the Republicans and Democrats in the United States.

Happiness Declassified

The advantages of inclusive dialogue are enormous. If we practice it, we will be able to get along better with others and become more intelligent and more flexible. And if we persevere, we'll start seeing spectacular results in no time. Let's be really smart and admit that we are all asses but wonderful.

In this chapter we learned that:

· Our dialogue is generally poor. We insist on imposing our views on others, which leads to arguments and the other party digging their heels in.

· Inclusive dialogue is a technique that involves:

a) recognising the other person's truth;

b) offering our view;

c) including the other person in our lives.

· *Recognising the other person's truth* consists of understanding how they think and the good points they have.

· When it comes to *offering our view*, we will try to include the other person's truth in our own, making it an extension of ours.

17
Learning to Say "No"

One day, the king brought his falconer two magnificent falcon chicks that had been given to him. With high hopes, he ordered him to train them to hunt.

A few months later, the falconer handed him a perfectly trained falcon but told him that the other one was defective and unable to learn. It had not moved from its branch since the day it arrived; it didn't hurt, and it had to be fed cut-up food.

The king summoned all of the kingdom's healers, but no one could make the bird fly. Infuriated, he issued an edict offering a reward to anyone who could manage it.

The next morning, from his chamber window, the king saw the falcon flying gracefully through the palace gardens.

"Bring me the person responsible for this miracle," the king requested.

And, to his surprise, a simple peasant was brought before him.

"How did you make the falcon fly? Was it some kind of magic?"

Awed, the man replied, "It was not difficult, Your Majesty. I just cut the branch, and the bird, rather than fall to the ground, began to fly."

In the psychology world, there are entire treatises on the thorny subject of knowing how to say "no." Many people find it hard to refuse others. Apparently, the Japanese are especially susceptible to this difficulty, and it complicates their lives.

But the fact is we are all affected by this problem at some time. Friends who ask us for money, relatives who invite us to baptism, requests that we find difficult to turn down and which we end up accepting only because we don't know how to say no. And again and again, we find ourselves regretting having loaned that money or going to an absurd ceremony dressed in a suit we hate.

Let's look at some cognitive principles that will help us improve our ability to say no. In essence, it is about understanding that:

a)   No one can make anyone else happy

b)   The best thing we can give to others is joy

c)   Fibbing is part of life

d)   Accepting a "no" is the best proof of friendship

NO ONE CAN MAKE ANYONE ELSE HAPPY.

This is one of the fundamental principles of rational psychology: no one can make anyone else happy. And knowing this underpins our ability to say no.

As we've seen, good mental health is founded on a deep awareness that we need very little to be happy. Once our basic needs are met, happiness is wholly in the mind – we either activate it to feel great or we don't. It's entirely up to us.

A mistake we often make is to think that, if we visit Grandpa at the old people's home, we'll make him happy. Wrong!

 Grandpa's fulfillment is entirely up to him, to his mind. A truly strong person doesn't need emotional crumbs from anyone else. And for weak individuals, there aren't enough kindnesses in the world to bring them out of their depression.

Adults – starting from the age of twelve – no longer need others. And that's great! Because from then on, we have an enormous capacity to enjoy ourselves and cooperate, to love and share – without absurd dependencies!

The fact that "no one needs anyone" means that doing favors or meeting others' expectations is unnecessary. People who ask us for things don't *need* them, whether they know it or not. We can refuse with complete peace of mind. Their happiness does not depend on it.

JOY, THE BEST GIFT

On the other hand, the best help we can give someone is to be radiant and happy and pass on some of this energy. This shows the way to a strong mind by example. And that means taking care of yourself.

Instead of thinking that grandpa needs you, think that he only needs to activate his own strength of mind; show him with your optimism, your rationality, that he can do it too with his own powers, which are the only ones that count. When you meet for lunch or a walk, show him with your smile how good it is to be alive. Let's not fall into the irrational misconception that something other than our own minds plays a role in our happiness.

For these two reasons – no one needs anyone else, and the best gift is joy – we can say no at any time in our lives because nobody needs our help. We can also say yes and be altruistic, but as we'll see below, these will be acts of cooperation, not arrogant assistance.

NGOs

When I present these rational ideas in public, I'm often asked about NGOs since these organizations are dedicated to *aid*. I think we have to be very careful with them because they sometimes engage in irrational behavior.

From a cognitive point of view, no one needs anyone else – except young children, of course. African countries, for example, do not need help, nor do the homeless, drug addicts, or the unemployed. Nor should anyone have to lend them any assistance. Humans are like any other free animal – we are more than capable of obtaining everything we need. Each and every one of us! Justice is another matter that *is* in our interest!

The ideal way to help the Third World would be to stop plundering it, installing puppets in its governments, and fomenting wars. But that's not help – it's justice, love, and rationality, which is where

NGOs could do an excellent job. It's better to go to the root of the problem than to put sticking plasters on open wounds.

But many people at NGOs love to think they are helping the "needy," like a gift from God, and that makes them feel superior. This is a neurotic approach.

Another example is the unemployment benefits we have in Spain. These are healthy mechanisms that we organize collectively to help our transition from one job to another, so they are not "aid" but a form of "cooperation."

Cooperation is another matter. That, I do like! I've worked for free in cooperative organizations. For a while, I lent a hand in a hostel for homeless people, most of them serious alcoholics. And I can assure you that what I got from them was much more than what I gave them. I learned a lot from those people, from their way of life, from their problems. I also made some amazing friends among the other volunteers. At no time did I feel that I was "helping" anyone: I was learning and doing social work that I might need one day.

And the same applies to my beloved organization the Voluntarios de Sant Joan de Déu, Barcelona's children's hospital. I provide training to them from time to time, but in reality, I consider it to be an exchange for the work they do: I teach them keys to rational cooperation, I meet wonderful people, and finally, I contribute to a service that my own family might need one day.

I know that distinguishing "help" from "cooperation" isn't easy, but it's worth the effort because the underlying philosophy changes everything. Let's break it down:

- Cooperating involves having a good time, growing, and learning.
- Cooperating avoids doing things for others that they could do themselves.
- Cooperating implies that the other person is strong and gives a lot in return.
- Helping, on the other hand, implies that the other person doesn't know or isn't able, that we're superior to the recipient or that they're dependent on those "helping" them.

One clear example of harmful help is those mothers – and I have met many – who go to great lengths to do everything for their children beyond a reasonable age, to always have them tied to their apron strings, hostages to their help. These mothers secretly want their children to never grow up. With their overprotective behavior, they raise neurotic and dependent children.

Confused Responsibilities

In many families, this kind of harmful help is constant, and it ends in a scenario of confused responsibilities. Let me give an example.

A mother wakes her son every day to go to school, even though he's twelve years old now. One day the boy asks her to wake him up an hour early because he has an exam and wants to revise. The mother forgets and wakes him at the usual time. The youngster flies into a rage.

"What a mess! I told you to get me up an hour earlier! Now I'm going to fail the exam! You're the worst!"

More than once, I've advised these youngsters, "Hey, you know what? If you don't want this to happen again, take care of your own affairs. No one knows better than you what's most important at any given time."

Young– and older – people should not be helped if it prevents them from learning the skills they need; this is essential in education. We must let them be fully responsible for their decisions and learn through experience. Of course we can give advice, but let them find their own way in life. They can accept it or not. That's what freedom is all about.

In dysfunctional, overprotective families, there tend to be a lot of overlapping responsibilities. For example, if the husband has an affair, the mother tells her twelve-year-old son with tears in her eyes about the problem. When the mistake is pointed out to her, she makes the excuse, "It's just that I needed support!"

These mothers would do well to understand that their child has no responsibilities in such matters. She must take care of her own problems and the son his. Overlapping responsibilities in the family are not good for anyone.

But of course, because, in their personal philosophy, they believe that everyone needs everyone all of the time because they have so many needs in the end, the family is rife with confusion, weakness, artificial obligations, criticism, and demands. Everyone weakens everyone else.

Drinking and Whoring

I love my father. He's kind like a few others. He couldn't be more likable. But if he decided now, at his seventy-six years of age, to start drinking heavily and using prostitutes, I would have no objections. It's his life and his sovereign decision! Of course, I wouldn't fund his escapades. I think I would try to understand the reason for his going astray and would probably suggest alternatives, but if he persisted in it, I would hug him and ask him to put his adventures in writing. I doubt they would be boring!

We're all free to choose our path in life. Who says my father should live like a Carthusian monk? Is that the recipe for happiness? It isn't. And what if it was! My father has the right to be unhappy if that's what he wants.

When we help someone, we usually try to impose our worldview on them, and that means placing restrictions on the recipient's freedom. If I gave my father a monthly allowance of 2,000 euros, I don't think I would let him waste it on whores and drugs. Harmful help always seeks to impose the ideological path of the helper. Instead of helping in this way, it's better to cooperate and let everyone make their own decisions and bear the consequences.

BLESSED FIBS

There's a phrase whose author I don't recall, which I like to repeat: "To be at peace with yourself, you must tell yourself the truth; to be at peace with others, you don't."

Thank goodness we know how to lie! In fact, people who don't know how – people with Asperger's syndrome, for instance – can encounter problems because they might say to an overweight girl they just met, "Wow, you're so fat; I've never seen anyone so big!"

Now and then, we have to tell a fib or two simply because the world isn't perfect – nor will it ever be! We're not all as mature as we would like to be, and we're easily offended. We behave foolishly, get angry, and have a myriad of neurotic reactions. It's normal.

If we're intelligent and flexible, we know that it's stupid and counterproductive to tell the WHOLE truth ALL of the time. In this sense, when it comes to saying no, little fibs are our friends. A lot of people prefer an "indirect" refusal to the blunt truth.

Another principle of rational psychology is that you don't have to demand anything from yourself, so let's resort to fibs with total peace of mind. If we're asked for help with a house move, it's fine to say that we have to work all weekend. In most cases, the other person will guess that it's untrue but would prefer a gentle lie to the hard truth.

GOING BACK ON YOUR WORD ISN'T SO BAD.

Going back on your word is not a very wise habit. I know. There are exceptions, however.

Perhaps because of our difficulty saying no, we've agreed to something we don't want to do. My advice is to write a message with an excuse and back out with a clear conscience. The other person may be angry at the change of plans, but that's life – it's imperfect. In any case, we often give in to our tiresome friend. Now, he deserves to be sent a message undoing an agreement for being so tiresome. And though it's much better to learn to say no, sometimes we find ourselves in situations in which it's better to backtrack, so let's fine-tune our ability to make excuses and pull out of an agreement. If the other person is rational, they will understand our maneuver. If not, it's their problem; they should relax.

ACCEPTING A "NO" AS PROOF OF FRIENDSHIP

A final strategy for learning to say no is to see refusals as wonderful proof of friendship. It's about saying to yourself, "If my friend really loves me, they won't mind me refusing them this or that." A true friend is motivated not by self-interest but by love. If denying them something material makes them angry or they withdraw their friendship, it's a false friendship. In which case, why maintain the relationship?

Saying "no" to someone puts their friendship to the test. In this sense, denying them favors is great.

ENDING A RELATIONSHIP

I am often asked how to end a relationship while causing as little damage as possible. My advice is to make it clear when ending it that a "no" to being a couple opens an incredible door to being great friends in the same way that we deny a favor to a friend but open up a thousand ways to cooperate.

I know that the "post-relationship friendship" is often mentioned and it's no comfort, but that's because it's not a sincere, heartfelt proposal. As we will see below, if, after being in a relationship, we devote ourselves to building the best friendship in the world, it will hurt less for the other person.

The pain of being abandoned comes precisely from telling themselves they've been abandoned, that all is lost. But if we persuade them that, with the change, they will gain a solid friendship for life, it's a different story.

I recommend saying – and feeling – something like:

Dear life partner, I'm grateful for the wonderful moments we have had together. They have given me a lot. I've gained so much from this relationship! Let's change the way we give to each other now. I propose that, from now on, we establish a fantastic friendship, one like a few others. Forever. And I couldn't be more serious! Our friendship is going to be a fundamental commitment for me!

We will have each other as unconditional support (as spurs and catapults) so that our lives are super fulfilled. I'll be by your side in every project so you carry it through with strength and joy. You will also have me to comfort you when you're sad and share your joys. You will never have known such a friendship! I promise you it will be worth it!

I pledge that no future partner will affect our fraternal relationship. To be with me, they will have to agree to this condition. I will not allow anyone to jeopardize our friendship.

One of the reasons it hurts so much when someone leaves us – sentimentally speaking – is that we believe it's all or nothing, but if we transform our relationship into an extraordinary friendship, we won't experience this feeling of total loss because it won't be there.

And why do we do this nonsense of erasing past relationships, of making them disappear? If we kept them as essential assets of our life, it would be wonderful: no one knows us better than our ex-partner! Few friends can love us more!

THE ENGAGEMENT RING

It was me who ended my most recent relationship. We went for dinner; I explained my reasons, and I proposed forging the best friendship in the world. And, to seal it, I gave her a ring that I'd bought a few days before.

Much as we give a ring to symbolize our commitment to sentimental love, why not give one when we end a relationship to express our desire for future love at an even more crucial time? I'm certain that couples who separate would avoid the hatred, painful divorces, and rows over the children if they were able to make a commitment to fraternal love.

A MOTHER'S LOVE

A patient once asked me the following question:

"Rafael, you always say life is beautiful, even that it couldn't be any more so! But what about the small tragedy of losing a mother? When you say goodbye to the person who loves you most, don't you lose a unique source of unconditional love?"

The question made me reflect. It's true that a mother's love is unconditional because it's total devotion. Almost all mothers would give their lives for their children, and we are unlikely to find that in a friend or partner.

I mulled over this for a few days. I was walking in the mountains, and I thought, *If a mother's love is a unique and wonderful thing, why on earth don't we practice it more? Why don't we extend it to more people? Why do we limit ourselves to one person instead of multiplying it?*

Since then, I have tried to love my friends, family, and ex-girlfriend as if *I* were their mother. Why not?! Being able to have such a great and intense interest in someone can only benefit us. Being capable of risking our lives for others is beautiful and binds us to them in a unique way.

That doesn't mean giving everything to them – much as a good mother doesn't spoil her child – but it does mean making a firm commitment to loving them unconditionally, including them in our lives forever, supporting them, and standing up for them.

In short, loving like a mother involves making our close friends an integral part of ourselves, parts of our body. This devotion multiplies and expands us; it makes us more than just one person; it makes us multiple beings with almost unlimited power!

Nothing prevents us from being able to love our ex-partners like a mother. With this new commitment, there will be no feeling of abandonment. And we will all win a new way of understanding relationships after a breakup and, why not, human relationships in general.

In this chapter we learned that:

- The keys to learning to say "no" are:
a) No one can make anyone else happy.
b) The best thing we can give to others is joy.
c) Fibbing is part of life.
d) Accepting a "no" is the best proof of friendship.
- Misplaced help is doing someone's else's work; it's better if we each make our own decisions and take charge of our own responsibilities.
- Cooperating means joining forces, creating collaborative mechanisms, without anyone imposing their ideology.
- Ending a relationship between two people after a breakup is a waste. It's better to begin a new relationship of deep friendship.

18
Revolutionizing Yourself with Love

A famed philosopher was set to debate with Nasreddin. On the appointed day, at the agreed time, he knocked on Nasreddin's door. There was no answer. The mullah had forgotten their engagement and was at the tea house playing checkers.

The longer he waited, the more agitated the philosopher became. Finally, before leaving, he took a piece of chalk and wrote on the door, "Stupid oaf."

As soon as he arrived at his house and saw the writing, Nasreddin ran to his guest's house.

"I am very sorry! I completely forgot our appointment," he said. "I only remembered when I arrived home and saw that you had written your name on my door."

A few years ago, Madrid witnessed the emergence of the *indignados* ("outraged") movement. In the wake of the banking crisis, a permanent camp was set up on Puerta del Sol, the capital's iconic square and ground zero of the Spanish road system. People were protesting against the corruption and incompetence of politicians. Many aligned themselves with the movement after reading the book *Time for Outrage!* by the French political activist Stéphane Hessel.

I would have joined had I been younger and more neurotic, but I was lucky enough to know rational psychology. And after studying

Gandhi, Epictetus, Albert Ellis, or Diogenes I could not accept the mad feeling known as "outrage" in myself.

I acknowledge the good intentions of the people who gathered on Puerta del Sol, and I support most of their arguments, but the problem is that "being outraged" is never the solution. Getting angry or yelling is always a form of madness; it's catastrophizing.

Getting angry is the easiest thing in the world: chimpanzees and orangutans are masters of the technique. Maintaining philosophical maturity and analytical ability, on the other hand, is reserved for the most intelligent humans.

If we want to be serene and rational people, we cannot let ourselves be carried away by outrage. Anger is the specialty of the mentally disturbed. Severe alcoholics – whose brains have turned to mush – fly off the handle day in, day out, making some spectacular scenes. There is no merit in knowing how to get angry: all it takes is having a few damaged neurons.

WORKING WITH LOVE, NOT ZEAL

In my first book, *Shake it Off!* I talked about dog muck. Barcelona, the city where I live, is beautiful, but its streets are covered in feces. Even the charming Eixample district is strewn with canine deposits.

A comedian I admire, Javier Cansado, was speaking on the radio one time about this thorny issue and said, "It's an absolute disgrace!

The owners should be forced to pick up the shit with their mouths! What a lack of common courtesy!"

But remarks like this take us down the path of neurosis. I know because I used to make them, too. Like Javier Cansado, I couldn't understand why I had to put up with other people's dogshit. It also seemed like the neighborhood dogs had a predilection for my front door.

The dog poohs don't bother me as much anymore. In fact, they don't smell as bad as human ones. It's just some organic waste – no big deal. But, in any case, being outraged is never the solution. If I ever decide to help change the situation, I might set up an association to solve the dog muck problem across the country. And I would have a great time: I would meet other volunteers, make friends, cooperate with the mayor, look at how to raise awareness about the issue. But if I decide not to work on it, I will choose not to attach much importance to it. To cognitively support our acceptance of the dog shit problem, we can consider that, in India, the problem isn't limited to animal crap: there, it's human excrement that accumulates in the streets. And it doesn't stop people from being happy. So, can I be happy here? Of course, I can!

Because joy, love, and good health are much higher values than justice and comfort.

HOW TO FACE ADVERSITY

There's a phrase they use in Alcoholics Anonymous meetings as a motto for personal growth. It's a good antidote to outrage: "God, grant me the serenity to accept the things I cannot change, The courage to change the things I can, And the wisdom to know the difference."

GANDHI, THE TEACHER

Mahatma Gandhi's concept of non-violence consists of making a commitment to removing aggression from one's life so that love prevails, relinquishing comfort, justice, status, or any advantage if it means using violence.

Gandhi taught us that we can demand anything, provided we do it through love. The Indian activist demonstrated that non-violence – persisting with love – can be much more effective than violence. In fact, he achieved Indian independence without firing a single shot, only through peaceful marches. And faced with Britain's aggression, he responded with brave and determined love. Nothing more and nothing less.

We can imitate Gandhi and practice non-violence in our personal and social lives. For example, by refusing to vote for any political measure that involves the use of violence, torturing citizens or punishing entire peoples, armed defense, and only accepting the use of persevering love. And if it means we lose the comfort in which we live, who needs it? We'll lose comfort but gain mental health and personal fulfillment.

THE SYSTEM THAT FEEDS THE PROBLEM

We often forget that conflicts are almost always systemic. What does this mean? Conflicts, adversity and failures have multiple causes – not just one – interacting bidirectionally.

We tend to like simple explanations, even if they don't make sense. We think, "Let's not add multiple factors into the analysis. It's better to explain it with just one", "Find one culprit, not lots," and "Design a solution, not a combination of solutions." This simplification is a big mistake because there are countless problems that can't be explained in such a way – sometimes, there isn't a linear cause-effect relationship, but influences that come and go, and several people or groups are involved. To solve problems, we have to think in a multivariate way.

For example, many years ago, I worked externally for a psychology book publisher. I met the director, and he seemed a pleasant and cultured person. At the first work meeting I attended, we were all around a large table, and the director started discussing issues with each of those present:

"Manuel, how are acquisitions going?"

"I'm a few authors short..." Manuel replied with his eyes down. "Are you saying they haven't all been signed yet? What a mess! I can't delegate anything to you! I'm sick of your incompetence!"

To my horror, the director barked at poor Manuel for ten more minutes. When he'd finished, he turned to someone else, and there was a similar scene. Finally, it was my turn, and he said, "Rafael, I'll speak to you next week because you haven't started work yet."

Phew, I'd dodged a roasting. But I realized that that director was an unbearable ogre and that, next week, I could expect the same treatment. When I came out of the meeting, I spoke to his secretary, a very sweet young woman.

"Hey, is the boss always like that?"

"Yes! I take tranquilizers because, if I didn't, I'd have gone crazy by now," she replied.

If I wanted to avoid this man's bad temper, I had to do something, and I considered the situation from a systemic point of view. As I said before, psychology teaches us that many problems are systemic in nature. That is, they are formed and maintained by systems of circular relationships or feedback.

$$A \rightleftarrows B$$

In the meeting, I had seen that the boss asked the questions, and the employees, scared, replied succinctly, barely looking him in the eye. They had the normal reaction of someone wanting to avoid danger. They thought, "I just want this to be over!" But it was precisely this reaction that increased the director's suspicion, insecurity, and aggression. He must have thought, "They're hiding something from me because they're inept layabouts! I'll have to wrench it from them!" In other words, there was a systemic relationship like this:

I decided to introduce a change in this circular interaction and set in motion a disruptive strategy. The director was flaring up because he was being dodged, so I would over-report to him. And that's what I did: the day after the awful meeting, I started sending him five emails a day with queries about my tasks: "What do you think if we choose such-and-such an author for this type of text?" And he would reply, "Very good, Rafael. That author could do a great job. Offer him

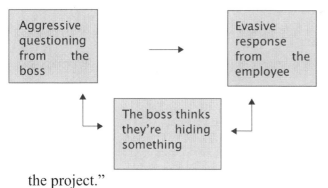

the project."

A few hours later, I would go to him with another query. In reality I knew what I was doing, but I didn't want him to get the impression I was avoiding him – quite the opposite! At the end of the day, after those five emails, I called him twice on the phone with more questions and clarifications.

That's what I did all week: by the end, I had written him twenty-five emails and called him fourteen times, until on the last day, he told me in an email, "Rafael, you're doing a great job. You can make your own decisions. You don't need to consult me so much!"

Perfect! I had achieved what I intended: he was fed up with my questions. Now, I just had to see if my plan would be successful at the meeting, which was the next day.

Once again, we sat at the big meeting table, and the rounds began. I watched him dish out the same scoldings as the week before. But when it was my turn, the miracle happened. The boss said, "Ah! I won't ask Rafael because I already know he's doing everything very well."

It was such a change that the publishing house staff suspected I was a relative of the boss, which was why he was treating me differently. But it was nothing like that. The miracle worked thanks to a systemic analysis of the problem, something we don't usually do when faced with conflict.

Whenever we have a problem with someone, we should consider that there may be several forces at play and we are involved. In politics, everyone has a role in the difficult situations that arise, and between us all, we can change them. If we get used to thinking this way, we won't get so angry, and we won't be outraged. It's more effective to seek solutions that involve everyone.

This poem by D. H. Lawrence expresses the error of outrage:

A SANE REVOLUTION

If you make a revolution, make it for fun,

don't make it in ghastly seriousness,
don't do it in deadly earnest,

do it for fun.
Don't do it because you hate people,

do it just to spit in their eye.
Don't do it for the money,

do it and be damned to the money.
Don't do it for equality,
do it because we've got too much equality,
and it would be fun to upset the apple-cart

And see which way the apples would go a-
rolling.
Don't do it for the working classes.

273

Do it so that we can all of us be little aristocracies on our own

and kick our heels like jolly escaped asses.

Don't do it, anyhow, for international Labour.

Labor is the one thing a man has had too much of.

Let's abolish labor; let's get done with laboring!

Work can be fun, and men can enjoy it; then, it's not labor.

Let's have it so! Let's make a revolution for fun!

HOW TO MAKE A REVOLUTION

A rational revolution, whether to get rid of the dog pooh or gain a country's independence, would need to meet the following requisites:

- Put it in a positive light: enjoy the process, learn with the project, work, and have a great time.

- Include adversaries in the growth process: persuade them that they will also learn and benefit from the change.
- Offer love every time adversaries lose their minds.
- Never catastrophize – exaggerating the negatives of a situation only makes us suffer.

I am not a separatist or a nationalist, but I would frame the Catalan claim for independence differently. To begin with, I would work to persuade the Spanish people that voluntary unions are the best kind. If Spain takes a step forward in that direction, it will become one of the most modern states in the world, on a par with Canada and the United Kingdom, which allow any consultation on secession. Civilized unions can be dissolved if one of the parties so wishes. Just like modern marriages can. And that's okay! In fact, freedom is stimulating and encourages each of the parties to always try to make the other happy.

I would advise the Catalan independence movement to never demand anything, because that involves violence. It's much better to argue with love that it's great to be modern, open and guarantors of the right to separate. Any consultation on independence is a good idea, as is any consultation on adhesion.

Equally, the State could try to persuade Catalans that a national union is the best thing. In other words, to suggest – not demand – the continuity of the union in a free and loving way. Wouldn't it be wonderful if a union for common happiness were proposed? Instead of making demands of the Catalan Government, it could put forward new, creative forms of cooperation.

Normally, fear is what prevents us from being rational. In this case, a fear of losing the opportunity to have self-determination in Catalonia and a fear of losing an economically powerful region in Spain.

As we have seen throughout this book, fear is overcome by letting go. Of course, Spain could be happy if it lost an economically strong region; it would see its material assets depleted, but it would gain in moral strength, love, and joy. The same goes for Catalonia: it could be immensely happy even if it were denied the ability to leave the national union; we can all learn to focus on what we have and not on what we don't have.

In the meantime, each could try to convince the other of their respective views. And, at the same time, love each other: sane or insane, because we all have both facets in our DNA: madness and good health.

CLEANING UP THE CRAP: A FASCINATING BUSINESS

We started this chapter with the unpleasant issue of dog muck. We're going to return to it now. Barcelona is a beautiful city, but the truth is its inhabitants can't claim to be civil. We still have a lot to learn in this regard. As I said before, the crap in question doesn't bother me anymore, but it would be great if the streets were cleaner.

Walking in the mountains one day, I came up with a fun and, I think, very effective solution: the doggy skewer. The idea is to provide all residents with what we could call a "civility set": a biodegradable bag and a sharp stick. We could distribute it to their mailboxes along with a letter explaining what to do:

> Dear neighbor,
>
> This civility set that you have just received is a weapon of social transformation. It consists of a doggy skewer and a bag, and it's for picking up any dog pooh you see on the street. Skewer the pooh with the stick and put it in the bag, then place it in the nearest bin.
>
> By doing so, you will contribute to making the streets more pleasant and, at the same time, show the way to the people who still don't take responsibility for their animals' waste. Teaching each other with love is an act of civility and personal growth. We all do bad things, and we can all learn to stop doing them. With joy and generosity, in Barcelona we will become champions of civility.

The doggy skewer experience could be marvelously instructive. The aim is to put into practice the main ideas of cognitive psychology:

a) To stop complaining about adversities, which makes them sources of unhappiness.

b) Put happiness above any advantage or comfort.

c) Understand that we're all a bit mad and, at the same time, wonderful.

d) Understand that the best way to influence others is to offer suggestions with love.

The initiative to clean up the city's dog muck would avoid exaggerating the world's imperfections and, what's more, if we all picked up one pooh a day, there would be no trace of them. Once the city was clean, it would be much easier for people to be more civil because a virtuous circle would be created. When a space is beautiful, we tend to respect it.

And what a lesson it would be for the people who don't pick up their dog muck to see their neighbors doing it even though it's not their responsibility. It would be a lesson in civility that would make an incredible impression on them. Whenever they saw a person using a doggy skewer, they would think to themselves, "If they can pick up poohs that aren't theirs, am I going to be so uncivil as to not pick up mine?"

But the most interesting thing about the "civility set" is that it would prompt many people to practice non-violent coexistence: they would stop complaining, be immensely understanding of others, and love them despite everything.

The experience would serve as a model of social influence for our friends, families, children, or colleagues. I believe that a city in which its citizens smile in the mornings and pick up a pooh that's not theirs is the best city in the world. The aim is to find imaginative solutions instead of complaining. If everyone gets used to this kind of response when there's a problem, wouldn't we find creative and effective solutions in every situation?

But the essential thing is not to get stupidly upset over minor things, to understand that mistakes tend to be systemic problems and there are always fun solutions that contribute to everyone's growth. Because we're all the same: we can all be heroes one day and villains the next; great geniuses in one thing and great fools in another. And deep down, a light illuminates us all. The light of unconditional love.

In this chapter we learned that:

- Outrage is a form of catastrophising or neurosis.
- Truly intelligent people accept the world's imperfection.
- *Fighting* for rights is feast today, famine tomorrow: we will gain advantages but lose mental health.
- It is much more effective to work on solutions through happiness than through anger.
- Many problems are systemic, and their solution requires an intelligent analysis that goes far beyond looking for a culprit.

19
Self-care

Rabbi Meir Cohen had devoted his entire life to studying the Scriptures. He was an authority appreciated throughout the world, and his sermons, especially the ones on the sin of speaking ill of others, were published in many languages.

On one occasion, he was returning home on a train and met another passenger, who told him about the purpose of his trip. "I'm going to the capital to meet the great rabbi Meir Cohen."

The rabbi was amused by the coincidence and wanted to find out more about how people thought of him. "And why do you call him a 'great rabbi'? What's so special about him? I think he's just a man like anyone else."

"How dare you be so rude about a peerless sage?" the passenger exclaimed as he gave him a resounding slap.

Days later, in the city, Meir Cohen gave a lecture at the university. In the end, the train passenger approached him, embarrassed, to apologize. He had turned white with shame when he realized that he had slapped the very hero he wanted to defend.

"Lord! What have I done? I have behaved unforgivably!" he said.

"There's nothing to forgive because you taught me something vital: the importance of not speaking ill of anyone, and particularly of oneself."

People become neurotic by being over-demanding. We demand too much of ourselves, of others, and of the world.

When we're the ones who make a mistake, we say to ourselves, "I'm a complete failure; I'm worthless!"

When it's everyone else who's wrong, we behave like the Taliban: "Everyone should treat me well all of the time!"

And when it comes to the world, we feel like EVERYTHING must ALWAYS work as planned. If it doesn't, it puts us in a foul mood.

But of these three families of neuroses, the first is the worst because self-castigation undermines self-esteem and leads to depression.

In this chapter, we will learn to take care of ourselves: that is, to always treat ourselves with understanding and love. We're going to stop punishing ourselves because it's counterproductive: it doesn't improve us, and it makes us weak.

"I'M A PIECE OF SHIT."

Many young people between the ages of twenty and thirty castigate themselves savagely for not being successful. I've seen many of them at my practice. They consider their jobs to be degrading and feel they haven't met the expectations they had. This self-castigation makes them suffer: their self-esteem is low, and they prevent themselves from enjoying their work.

They also have a terrible time when they're with their friends. They compare themselves to them and always come away feeling defeated. Sometimes, they even stop seeing their group to avoid this feeling of worthlessness.

More than once, I've been told, "Rafael, I'm such a failure." Or straight up, "I'm a piece of shit." They don't realize it, but it's not success or failure but the absurd demands they place on themselves that are making them truly unhappy. And, paradoxically, it contributes to them not fulfilling their potential.

Their real handicap is their all-or-nothing mentality, which increases their fears because it continually traps them between a rock and a hard place. If they stopped making demands of themselves, they would immediately begin to shine, naturally, almost without realizing it.

At the age of twenty-seven, I was seized by these mad demands on myself. I went to a psychologist because I was unhappy: I punished myself for failing to achieve certain goals.

I had been an exemplary student and a brilliant PhD candidate, but after a few years of lecturing in the faculty, I went into a tailspin and gave it all up. I was pushing thirty and found myself enmeshed in a university rife with political wrangling, my future precarious and uncertain. But, most of all, I felt like I was letting everyone down, especially myself.

Some of my friends were reaching important milestones in their work and I wasn't. I thought everyone was better than me. In one of my conversations with the psychologist, I said to her, "It's just that everyone is achieving their goals, and I'm not achieving any of them."

"Like who? Who around you has achieved more than you?" she asked me.

"My brother Gener, for one. He works for the council as a social worker," I replied.

"And that's a better job than yours? You're at the university, and though you may not have a permanent contract, you're a very good lecturer, and you translate important psychology books. I don't see much difference!" she exclaimed.

The truth is, at the time, I thought everyone was doing better than me, but what was actually happening was that my expectations of myself were somewhat excessive. And my values were wrong.

Fortunately, I soon began to cleanse my mind with cognitive psychology and realized that the only logical expectation to have of ourselves is to be *people who love*. Everything else is surplus. If we want to be strong and happy and do well, all we have to do is *love life* and *love others*.

DIABOLICAL SWIMMING

Being over-demanding almost always stems from childhood. Society, with its misconceived myths, inculcates it in us very early. I had a personal experience in my childhood that illustrates this brainwashing.

When I started school at the age of seven, I went to a Catholic institution in Barcelona. One of the subjects was swimming. My first day at the pool promised to be wonderful. Like all children, I loved the water, the sea, the bathtub! But it turned out to be a nightmare. I didn't know how to swim. The teachers, a couple that was like something out of the Soviet Union, formed us into a long line. And one by one, when our turn came, they threw us into the water. The method consisted of "catching" us by the head with a long metal stick with a hook on the end while we thrashed about.

Sure enough, we learned to swim. But also, to hate swimming. I still detest the smell of chlorine. How lucky were the kids who already knew how to swim! Their parents had taught them in a loving and rational way and not with the deranged method of hooking them by the neck.

It took me forty years to overcome my phobia of swimming pools (although, as it happens, I go to a pool that's disinfected with bromine and it doesn't smell). But, although finally, I like to swim, I'm not a good swimmer. Isn't it incredible that with all those years of swimming, the result was so poor? That pair of teachers certainly did a very mediocre job. Their work is a clear example of bad education.

Many still believe that being demanding of oneself – and others – is the key to good character and success. They think that brute force, bravery, or excessive demands are virtues when, in reality, they're signs of madness.

Good teaching is always fun and safe. All learning works much better through passion than through fear. Being over-demanding is self-sabotage. Flagellating oneself can achieve some things, but very little compared to love.

THE REFORMED BOXER

At the beginning of this book, I mentioned Allen Carr, author of *The Easy Way to Stop Smoking*. He is undoubtedly the best psychologist in the world, even though he never studied psychology or practiced it. In one of his books, he offers an anecdote that explains the stupidity of being over-demanding of oneself. When he was young, in chilly Scotland, he did boxing – at school! It was the fifties, and this form of madness was still practiced in physical education classes. As Carr was a very athletic boy, he learned to box very well and was a youth champion in his region for several seasons. But it wasn't until many years later, once he discovered his method to stop smoking rationally, that he was able to admit that he had hated boxing and that, more generally speaking, brute force, aggression, and self-flagellation were madness.

Boxing is an insane act that only shows what animals we can be. It's undoubtedly the height of stupidity to pretend that we can irrationally ignore fear. Not surprisingly, professional boxers give up boxing as soon as they can and never go back in the accursed ring. What a thing to enjoy!

But legends like John Wayne and Sylvester Stallone make us desire supposed virtues like toughness, guts, or willpower when flexibility, the ability to be passionate or the power of enjoyment are much better.

BASE CAMPS

The case of Eduardo, a boy who came to my practice a few years ago, illustrates the theme of this chapter: the usefulness of knowing how to take care of oneself.

Eduardo was a very intelligent child, exceptionally gifted. Likable, warm, fun. But at the age of eleven, he developed an obsessive disorder related to cleanliness. Specifically, he had to wash his hands continuously for fear of being contaminated. And three times a day, he performed a forty-five-minute tooth brushing and rinsing ritual. Otherwise, he felt like something bad would happen to his health.

Soon after starting therapy, he told me that he wanted to go camping with the school but that he didn't dare because of his problem with cleanliness. He was very agitated because he couldn't make up his mind. He explained, "We went last year. The sinks are in a communal area, and if they see me washing for so long, they'll think I'm really weird."

"And if you don't wash, you'll get agitated, will you?" I asked.

"Yes! I might not sleep all night!" he admitted.

"All right, so don't go to the camp. In a few months, thanks to the therapy, you won't have this problem, and then you'll be able to join your friends," I suggested.

"Oh! But how do I explain that I can't go? I'm so embarrassed," he said, almost in tears.

Whenever we have neuroses, not only do we suffer because of them, but we almost always also punish ourselves doubly for having them. Sure enough, two things were making Eduardo suffer: his obsession with cleanliness and being different, and this pressure increased his mania for cleanliness in a devilish loop.

In fact, in that session we couldn't work on the contamination and germs. We had to focus first on his self-esteem. And to do this I told him about my experience as a mountaineer. I explained to him what true courage consists of – something that is built through *base camps*.

"Have you ever seen a climber going up a mountain?"

"Yes! In the Himalayas. Edmund Hillary was the first to climb Everest!" he immediately replied.

"Exactly. Well, one thing that's essential for all the great climbers is what they call the base camp. They store food, clothes, communication devices and oxygen there in the tents. As they ascend, they establish more base camps. On a big expedition, like climbing Everest, there can be three or four base camps on the way to the summit. If the climbers run into difficulties, they return to base camp to rest, replenish supplies, and obtain weather information."

"Yes! I've seen it. They even cook spaghetti inside the tents!" he told me.

"Yes, of course. And meat and potatoes! But listen, no one tries to climb a big mountain without base camps! You see? Rational courage is about knowing how to take care of yourself, take it slowly, and set up safety nets – as many as you need! This is precisely what enables us to reach such remote places."

Eduardo understood me right away. The boy had always demanded a lot of achievements and abilities of himself, and it had led to an absurd *all-or-nothing* dichotomy. It was like a mountaineer saying, "If I don't climb Everest in one attempt, I'm a coward and a failure." But Eduardo learned that he didn't have to feel bad about not going to the camp, or if he decided to go, he could always go home if he got anxious. And, in both cases, he could fib to save face with his friends.

Because in emotional terms, setting up base camps means:

- Not feeling bad about being vulnerable or experiencing fears, no matter how irrational they may seem. We're all good for nothing! We fail, but we're also amazing.

- Learning how to subdivide difficult tasks into easier parts. No one learned to do quadratic equations without first mastering simple ones!

- Keep things simple whenever you can. For example, we all find it hard to say difficult things face-to-face, so write a note, email or WhatsApp message. The important thing is to communicate – let's not be our own Taliban.

- Giving ourselves a margin of error. In other words, having a plan B. If we meet someone for the first time and it's stressful, we can say we have a headache and leave. Always having a way out is smart. Demanding ourselves that we "be normal" is what makes us neurotic. Nobody is completely "normal".

- Fibbing. Healthy and compassionate lies are the oil that greases this imperfect world. We often need to save face with friends, bosses, or colleagues who are too demanding (a bit mad). A little lie can help us muddle through.

PERSEVERANCE AND HARD WORK

Sometimes, we insist on making things difficult for ourselves because we're afraid of being weak being unable to perform tasks with effort and perseverance. But nothing could be further from the truth. Perseverance and sustained effort are abilities that we can hugely enjoy, provided they're framed within a good self-protection strategy.

When I was young, I could spend eight straight hours studying a subject and enjoy the hard work. But these were tasks I knew how to do – they didn't involve absurd frustrations or mad battles with myself.

Taking care of yourself is not incompatible with improving, learning, working, and striving. In fact, it's when you feel safe and protected that you best explore the environment around you.

A TOAST TO PROZAC

Some of the most severe self-castigation happens when we punish ourselves for being neurotic. We say to ourselves, "I'm so hopeless! No one will ever put up with me!" Or, as one patient said to me, "I'm broken!"

Insulting ourselves in this way is irrational for many reasons. First of all, because it's pointless – all it does is lower our morale and prevent us from changing. Second, because neurosis is the disease of the twentieth century – more and more neurotics will populate the planet. And third, because we all have faults and that doesn't stop us from being brilliant as people who love.

How many great people – scientists, artists, rulers, philosophers – have been neurotic in many areas of their lives?

Take, for example, my admired Winston Churchill, the British Prime Minister, Nobel Laureate in Literature, and member of the House of Lords.

Happiness Declassified

Or one of the greatest scientists of all time, Charles Darwin, who developed the theory of evolution. He suffered from social phobia and hypochondria. He felt fortunate to have emotional limitations because they had pushed him to focus on his great passion: science. As soon as he married, he went to live in a peaceful retreat in the countryside, where he only left to go to spas to treat the stomach ailments created by his mind. His colleagues often came to visit him, and he turned them away. They knew that when he was going through a bad patch, it was better not to bother him.

Or better still, the man who, for many, is the foremost scientist in history, Isaac Newton. All by himself, he invented the infinitesimal calculus and achieved advances in the fields of optics, modern physics, and astronomy with his ingenious law of universal gravitation. Einstein only had one painting in his study and it was a portrait of Newton. Well, this superman of the sciences was tremendously neurotic: apparently, he never had sex, and he suffered from chronic insomnia, depression, hypochondria, fits of anger, amnesia, and various phobias. But that didn't stop him from reaching the pinnacle of physics. As the English poet Alexander Pope wrote, "God said, let Newton be! And all was light."

One of my best friends, Miquel, is a great artist. He possesses enormous sensitivity. A doodle of his on a napkin can leave you speechless. I've spoken to Miquel many times about how common neurosis is among artists. He told me once that, at a dinner with other painters in Paris, one of the most prominent artists raised his glass to make a toast and blurted out, "To Prozac!"

To which the others responded in unison: "To Prozac!"

BLESSED COOPERATION

Some patients tell me that they're afraid that their neuroses will prevent them from finding a partner. But this is an irrational fear because weakness is precisely the main driver of cooperation, union, and couples' relationships themselves. We interact because it's pleasant to do so, but also because cooperation allows us to overcome handicaps. In fact, if we were all extremely strong and happy, there would be very few couples; we would go from flower to flower, enjoying everything and everyone.

People who accept their weaknesses without embarrassment are the perfect candidates for a beautiful and lasting relationship because they know that their partner will be their closest collaborator. Having neuroses isn't a problem when it comes to finding a partner, quite the contrary. Charles Darwin, for example, had a happy marriage and a very pleasant family life with his ten children. His social phobia pushed him towards science, but also towards his family, which he valued above everything else. There's a rational reflection we often do at my practice. To take the pressure off ourselves, to learn how to take care of ourselves, we ask ourselves, "What if I always had anxiety? And was it never cured? Could I be happy? Could I do valuable things for myself and others? Could I adapt like Charles

Darwin, retire to the countryside, lead a life of family and science or art, and achieve a good level of fulfillment?"

The answer you have to give is, "Of course I can!"

SLOWLY BUT SURELY

Personal development is something that must be done slowly but surely. In other words, it must combine continuous work to banish all our fears with delightful self-care.

With this in mind, cognitive psychologists are in favor of anxiolytics and antidepressants because they are a way to take care of oneself while our mental development is underway, though it's wise to make limited use of them. Personal growth also requires us to face the situations that disturb us to some extent because then we can work on them.

For example, people who have generalized anxiety should avoid taking anxiolytics because it's those moments of tension that are the most useful time to work on the issue. This effort is what will cure them. But on the other hand, on an especially bad day, it might not be a bad idea to take an anxiolytic at the end of the day to get some rest.

In real life, the tortoise, slow but relentless, is much more effective than the mad hare. Let's never forget that taking care of ourselves is one of the keys to personal growth.

In this chapter we learned that:

- Being self-demanding is the fastest route to becoming neurotic because it's a mediocre means of motivation.
- The best personal development is exciting, safe and fun.
- Whenever we can, we should set up "base camps". In other words, to reach our goal, divide our efforts into simpler tasks, without forgetting to always have somewhere to retreat to, an exit.
- Weakness is nothing to be ashamed of. We're all weak; the smart thing to do is to accept it, find ways to compensate for it and imaginative solutions.
- Being neurotic is not bad in itself. For many famous people, their neuroses have helped them develop other facets.
- Emotional weakness is an engine for an enduring relationship with a partner because it makes their support even more beautiful and significant.
- Using anxiolytics and antidepressants at certain times can be a good way to take care of yourself.

20
Learning to Learn

A young man was walking from one village to another across a mountain range. At one point, a dense fog began to cover everything. The youngster picked up the pace to arrive sooner, but he tripped at a bend in the path and fell into the void.

As he fell, he desperately reached out and managed to grab hold of a branch. What luck! He had saved his life! But how would he get back up? The rock face was vertical. What's more, he couldn't see anything because of the fog.

Hanging from the branch in the middle of nowhere, he thought he was doomed, and he yelled, "God, help me!"

And suddenly, there was a voice in his mind, clear and thunderous. "Let go. Trust me."

He shook his head. He must be having a ridiculous hallucination. It was freezing, and night had fallen.

He yelled again, "If you exist, Lord, help me. I'm freezing to death!

And, again, the voice inside said, "Let go. Trust me."

Eight hours later, the day dawned, and some villagers passed on the same path. At the point where the young man had fallen, they found his stick. They peered over the edge of the path, and what they saw left them bemused: there the boy was, frozen to death, clutching a branch. And underneath him, there was not a void but another path, just a yard from his stiff, icy feet.

Because of the fog, he had not realized that there was no precipice, only another path through the mountains.

This story illustrates what I call the *non-existent precipice*. That is, the mistaken belief that we are no good at certain things, such as mathematics, dance, and studies false notions of inability that block us until we really do become incapable. These self-limitations happen a lot in the school or work environment, and they lead to many wasted opportunities.

For a long time, I was useless at maths. I always flunked. I hated numbers, and they felt the same about me. This awful relationship persisted for the first few years of my education until I decided in secondary school to take the bull by the horns, and for the first time in my life, I started passing exams. Accursed mathematics was beginning to cut me some slack. But as soon as I was given the opportunity, I moved on to "pure arts." Phew!

And then something happened that would change things forever between Pythagoras and me. At secondary school, I started giving private lessons to earn some pocket money. At the time, my family's finances were foundering, and if I wanted a pair of jeans or some notebooks I had to pay for them myself. And so, before I knew it, I became the best-known revision class professional in my neighbourhood. My diary was full of school-age customers.

And I had some great successes! There were two twins who went from flunking eight subjects to passing everything with B's and one or two A's.

The following year, when summer came, I decided to spend July and August concentrating on my tutoring business. My goal was to buy an electric guitar and an amplifier. I needed a lot of students to do this.

Then I got a call from a neighbor who was two years older than me:

"I hear you give revision classes and that you're very good. I need you! I've still got my third-year mathematics to do in September."

"Sorry, but I don't teach maths. In fact, I only did compulsory and second-year maths. In year three, I took 'pure arts,'" I explained.

"Rafael, I need you. I'm useless at maths! Take a look at it and explain it to me. I'll pay you double what you charge," she told me, certain I could do it.

The offer of double tempted me. I would have the guitar and amplifier in the bag, so I agreed. "We'll try, but I can't promise anything," I said.

When September arrived, Irene, as my neighbor was called, got a B on her exam, and thereafter, every level of secondary school maths became part of my portfolio of services.

Later, in the psychology faculty, I crossed paths with maths again, but I wasn't afraid of it anymore. I got the best grades in statistics and started working on various research projects for the lecturers.

Where had my childhood belief that I was useless at maths gone? It had disappeared! It's true that my strength had always been in the arts, abstract thinking, philosophy, and verbal reasoning, but the truth was that I wasn't bad at the sciences, either.

The "non-existent precipice effect" makes us believe foolishly that we're no good at a great many things. But almost everyone is good at almost everything. Learning is a lot of fun and easy if nothing scares us.

A PROFESSIONAL MOUNTAINEER

Not long ago, I had another episode of overcoming a limitation. For years, I had described myself as having no sense of direction, whether in the city or the mountains. When I went hiking, I would let someone else lead the way. I was convinced that my brain didn't function in that way, and the proof was that when I went out alone, I almost always got lost. But, once again, it was a made-up precipice.

I recently spent a fortnight alone walking a trail in the Pyrenees. At a shelter, having dinner with a mountaineer I had just met, we had the following exchange:

"I follow very detailed routes that I get online. I download them and put them in my GPS," he told me.

"Well, I use old-fashioned maps; I get on great with them," I replied, pulling one of them out.

"Wow! I can't get my head around those. I'm pretty bad at finding my bearings," he responded.

"It's really easy," I said. "With a good map and a compass, it's impossible to get lost. If you check your position every so often, you know where you are and where to head with a lot of accuracy. It's a blast!"

In the morning, when we said goodbye, and I started walking, I reflected on our conversation the night before. Unlike in the past, I now consider myself a good guide! And I liked orienting and maps! Clearly, I had overcome another non-existent precipice effect.

RESUMING LESSONS WITH JOY

Recently, a former patient named Tomás returned to the practice. He explained that his work situation had changed, and he felt unsettled. He had gone from being a firefighter – his lifelong profession – to a high-end car salesman. He told me he had been discharged from the fire service due to back problems and had accepted early retirement. He could work in other roles, so he had found a job at an important dealership.

It all started smoothly. His passion had always been cars, and he was outgoing and likable. He also found commission-based work stimulating. In fact, in just two months, he became the star salesman!

But then things took a turn and Tomás was considering leaving the job.

The management was now asking the sales staff to do some administrative tasks, arranging financing and other paperwork. Tomás was overwhelmed because he "hated" these tasks.

"I've always been useless at figures and paperwork. Give me some action! I'm on the verge of telling the manager I'm leaving."

"That would be a shame because your sales are doing very well, and that's the essential thing," I said.

"But I'm getting very stressed. And I don't enjoy the work anymore!"

Tomás was suffering from the non-existent precipice effect. In other words, he was limiting himself because of a mistaken early experience. Of course, he could learn everything necessary to do that part of the job! And even enjoy it!

I told Tomás about the possibility that he was blocking himself and suggested he change tack. What if it wasn't true that he was useless at figures and paperwork? What if learning to perform these tasks wasn't as difficult as it seemed? And if, in no time, he could start enjoying it all? Tomás accepted the challenge, and today he is the best car salesman in his region, and the part of the job that was so hard for him is now "a breeze," in his words.

My own experiences with self-limitation have led me to advise everyone to reassess their presumed weaknesses and set out to improve. But this time, with bags of excitement and joy and a good learning plan! They will find that they're not so bad at whatever discipline it is. It was a phantom they created for themselves!

Adults who can't swim or ride a bike spring to mind. It's curious how they sometimes allow years to pass before finally deciding to learn, and they all think it's going to be extremely hard.

I met a fifty-year-old woman, Nadia, who couldn't swim, even though she lived in Barcelona and loved going to the beach. During therapy, the subject happened to come up, and I asked her, "Hey, Nadia, have you ever considered learning?"

"Now and again, but I'm a bit old for it now, don't you think?" she replied.

"Are you serious? You're in good shape."

"Rafael, I can't be bothered to take lessons every week, and it must be really hard," she said sadly.

"Listen to me. Swimming is the easiest thing in the world because the body floats. You just have to be calm in the water and move your limbs a little to go forward. It's ridiculously easy!"

And she listened. She enrolled with a private coach at her neighborhood pool, and in two days, she was doing doggy paddling. Within a month, Nadia, who was very athletic, was swimming the crawl better than I could. She showed me in a video.

This is a perfect example of how we can spend years mistakenly believing that something is very difficult. And it's all out of fear: of making fools of ourselves, of looking silly.

BACK TO SCHOOL

The non-existent precipice effect is something that is currently exacerbated by our education systems. Because they're based on fear instead of enjoyment, young people begin to place limits on themselves as soon as a difficulty arises: "I'm terrible at maths," "I have a very bad memory," "I'm shy," etc.

Because of exams, kids focus on their virtues and hide their flaws. And so these hidden flaws become self-imposed gaps in their knowledge for the rest of their lives. And beware! Their virtues will never reach their full potential because kids rarely use the real fuel for learning, which is enjoyment. This leads to enormous educational waste.

But, as adults, we can largely reverse this damage if we:

a) Let go of any kind of self-limitation. Set out to achieve fabulous levels of mastery in everything that was taboo until now.

b) Tale all the pressure off ourselves. Understand that nothing is necessary. If we never learned to swim: screw swimming! And the same goes for maths and the rest of the world's knowledge. Out with our fears!

c) Let's always tap into the power of enjoyment in all our tasks.

OPENING OUR EYES LIKE AN OSTRICH

One of the most curious phenomena of self-limitations is that when we experience them, we perform the tasks "with our eyes closed." Because of our fear, we deal with the issue by avoiding it, and no one can learn that way. Tomás, the great car salesman, for instance, was so averse to the paperwork that he didn't give it much attention; he arranged the financing while looking the other way.

They say that ostriches bury their heads in the sand when they see a predator. I was very happy when a naturalist friend informed me that this was not the case.

"Rafael, how could that be true? If an animal did that, it wouldn't last two days. No animal does that." My friend paused, but funny and wise as he is, he added, "Oh, no. I'm wrong! There is one that does it: humans."

Sure enough, people are capable of doing things as stupid as drinking alcohol when they have a problem when what they should do is have a coffee and set out to solve the issue in the best possible way.

Most of the tasks we undertake are very easy to perform if we do them with our eyes open, that is! When facing a task we can't stand, I always recommend picking up a notebook. Write down any tricks, tips, and details that could make it easier. With our eyes wide open, pay attention to anything that might help. For example, in Tomás's case, he could write down things like, "Keeping a card with a plan of action for doing the paperwork will be great for me,"; "A checklist will ensure I don't forget anything"; "When I calculate the financing, I'll use a spreadsheet, so I don't make mistakes"; "If I go over the figures three times, it will be almost impossible to go wrong." ...

Remember, ostriches don't bury their heads because if they did, they wouldn't last two days. All animals have a command of their surroundings. And they experience no stress in their lives! We are also made to master our environment. Just one small detail is required: opening our eyes.

A GREAT LEARNING PLAN

So, when we find ourselves faced with a task that causes us discomfort, the solution is to assume that it's one of these non-existent precipices. And once the pressure is off, we must organize a learning project that's as fabulous as possible. This means:

- Planning it in good time. No one learns in a hurry; it's better to have a schedule that includes days for enjoyment.

- Being ambitious. The higher we aim, the more motivated we will be. For example, saying, "I'm going to learn to swim like a dolphin and have a 10/10 body," is much better than, "I'm going to try to resolve this issue that I have a complex about."

- Framing it in a great environment. For example, enrolling in a swimming course at a nice pool, practicing at the beach, buying fashionable swimwear, etc.

- Insisting on making it fun. Every time we get stressed, stop! There are a thousand ways to do it enjoyably. Let's not persist with using willpower at any cost.

- Keeping our eyes wide open. That is, keeping a notebook handy in which to write down tricks and tips. If there's a task we can't stand, it's because, through fear, we have always done it with our eyes closed.

In this chapter we learned that:

· When we say to ourselves, "I'm no good at this," he place stupid limits on ourselves. We can all get pretty good at almost any task.

· Our fear of making fools of ourselves underlies the non-existent precipice effect.

· We can avoid self-limitations if we don't accept them, take the pressure off ourselves and plan a beautiful learning experience.

· One condition for overcoming self-limitations is to focus on enjoyment.

· It is important to keep our eyes open and face the task that is unpleasant to us. We can help ourselves by writing down tricks or tips in a notebook.

Epilogue

I write these last lines from the terrace of my mountain refuge in Colungo, on the Sierra de Guara. The sun is going down, and an orange light blankets the horizon. The view of nature unfolding before my eyes tells me that life has a lot to offer us, so much that if we opened our minds to all of it, our brains wouldn't be able to take it in: they would overflow with so much pleasure, so much neural synchrony, as neurologists term it.

Ana Amalia Barbosa, the quadriplegic teacher, comes into my thoughts, her example opening a crack in my mind through which the certainty that we can all be as happy as we want seeps in.

Life offers endless possibilities for enjoyment, and here, as night falls in Colungo, I enter a state of abundance. I know I will be immensely happy until I die.

The mind is flexible, and if I practice with perseverance, my neurons will become accustomed to traveling the channels of harmony. Any emotional disturbance comes from a misconception, from a state of want, which is nothing more than smoke, absurd ideas that I can brush aside.

Over and over, I will insist on training my mind as if it were a young horse. Starting from the angry outbursts of neurosis, I will make my brain gloriously fluid so that it performs at its best.

With a cognitively oiled mind, I will strengthen all of my personal facets to a near-sacred level. I will be able to look back at my life and appreciate that it is great.

All my ups and downs – pleasures or adversities – will be adventures with which to grow and become stronger and happier. Even illness will be just another path to realization.

Dear reader, I am waiting for you on the road to rational fulfillment. It doesn't matter how long it takes to travel it, what matters is moving forward at a steady pace. Don't stop. You will build mental muscle, and life will open up in front of you like a cherry tree in blossom. Start polishing your mind. Tune in to harmony over and over again. Write poems at every turn. Try to never fight or be outraged. May discomfort be fertile ground for you. The planet will thank you for your new attitude to life and reward you with its many treasures.

I'll see you there.

Synopsis

Can we learn to be happy? The answer is yes. Can we be content in the face of adversity? Also yes.

How do we know this? Because millions of people do it: they're practically always happy and satisfied. There are some notable cases like the philosopher Epictetus, who was born a slave but decided to make the most of his opportunities and not complain.

This book describes the value system, the personal philosophy, of this kind of person. And guess what... we can all acquire this direction in life. Principles that affect every area of life: how we understand relationships, work, friendships, illness and even death.

The authors are mental and behavioral health practitioners with vast experience helping people become twenty-first-century Epictetuses. Literally thousands of their readers and patients are amazing examples of personal growth. Many of their testimonies can be seen online: people who found themselves gripped by fear and panic, by insecurity or shyness, by a lack of energy and indecision... And now they're shouting from the rooftops about their new state. They are strong and happy.

What you have in your hands is the most complete and in-depth cognitive-behavioral therapy manual produced.

You may think this news too good to be true. If so, read the book with an open mind and start applying everything it recommends.

Don't worry, within a few days—weeks, at most— you'll start to see it for yourself.

In first-century Imperial Rome, the philosopher Epictetus laid the foundations for cognitive-behavioral therapy. His most famous statement remains a bombshell: "We are not disturbed by what happens to us, but by our thoughts about what happens to us."

If my girlfriend leaves me and I sink into depression, it won't be because of the event itself, but because I'm saying to myself: "I'm all alone! I'll never find anyone else like her! I'm going to be such a miserable wretch!"

Our assessment of reality affects us: our judgements, our inner dialog. And all of this can be changed.

Some people go through a radical transformation after a near-fatal accident or life-threatening illness. They stop worrying about trivialities, they value all the little things in life, they focus on what's important... in other words, they radically change their mindset. Can we do something similar from the safety of our homes, without placing our health at risk? We certainly can: through reasoning, acquiring a deep personal philosophy.

****

The father of emotional illness is "terribleitis," the habit of telling oneself that any adversity is "terrible," "the end of the world," "nuclear Armageddon". We may even elevate to "terrible" minor things like stepping in dog crap or a co-worker saying something unpleasant to us.

This is neurosis: a skin-deep complaining mindset, inner complaining on the tip of our tongues.

But the strongest and happiest people never "terriblize". Like Stephen Hawking, the wheelchair-bound scientist. For almost all of his adult life, this amazing man suffered from ALS and could neither move nor speak, and yet he became one of the greatest scientists of all time, and most importantly, a very happy person.

Stephen knew that complaining is pointless and a waste of time. He also saw his paralysis as a minor inconvenience: "However difficult life may seem, there is always something you can do and succeed at."

Can we, too, abandon our terribleitis? Of course we can! The secret will be to argue forcefully against it, persuade ourselves that nothing is so terrible, that there are always opportunities for happiness.

****

NECESSITITIS

If the father of emotional illness is "terribleitis", the mother is "necessititis". The belief that we need a much more to be okay: a good job, success, money, a partner, home ownership, lots of friends, talents, being beautiful, smart, extroverted, slim, fit... and 10,000 other things!

And beware: if you fail in just one of these things, you consider yourself a failure, the worst species of worm!

The strongest and happiest people need very little to be happy. It's their most cherished secret. All they need is food and drink for the day. If their spouse leaves them, they think, "Ugh, I'm sad this has happened, but I still have arms and legs; there are a million valuable things I can do; I'm lucky because being single is also great."

At the end of his life, St. Francis of Assisi purportedly said, "Every day I need fewer things, and the few I need, I need very little of."

Every invented need is a burden. It's obvious. If I think that I absolutely need to succeed to be okay and, at some time, I don't manage it, I will make myself unhappy. And the same goes for everything else: work, comforts, even full health.

We hope you enjoy this book.

****

Made in United States
Troutdale, OR
11/16/2024

24908861R00173